Expanded 2nd Edition

easy Campfire cooking

250+ FAMILY FUN RECIPES FOR COOKING OVER COALS AND IN THE FLAMES WITH A DUTCH OVEN, FOIL PACKETS, AND MORE!

FOX CHAPEL
PUBLISHING

Photo Credits

Georgia Pellegrini (p. 3): Diane Cu

Catch of the Day, The Stick Way (pp. 12, 18): Carson Morgan

No-Crust Apple Pie (p. 23): Jessica Morris, *jessicalynette.com*

Basic S'more for 2 (p. 25): Brent Hofacker, via Shutterstock

Skewers and Kebabs (pp. 9, 27): Bonny Turayev, *violetssilverlining.blogspot.com*

Tropical Shrimp Skewers (pp. 1, 35): Dana DeVolk, *thissillygirlskitchen.com*

Lemon Chiffon Pie (p. 85): Heather Painchaud, *homemadeheather.com*

Breakfast Biscuits (p. 91): Tina Butler, *mommyskitchen.net*

Dutch Oven (p. 109): from *Dutch Oven & Cast Iron Cooking*, *foxchapelpublishing.com*

Caramel Apple Crisp (p. 120): Elizabeth Waterson, *confessionsofabakingqueen.com*

On a Grate (p. 121): BlacksmithCreations, *etsy.com/shop/blacksmithcreations*

Southwest Chicken (p. 124): Jothan Yeager

Beer Can Chicken (p. 125): Heather Nolan

All other photos: CQ Products, *cqbookstore.com*

© 2012, 2022 by Fox Chapel Publishing Company, Inc., 903 Square Street, Mount Joy, PA 17552.

Easy Campfire Cooking, 2nd Edition (2022) is a revised edition of *Easy Campfire Cooking* (2012), published by Fox Chapel Publishing Company, Inc. Revisions include new recipes and photographs.

Recipe selection, design, and book design © Fox Chapel Publishing.
Recipes and select photographs as noted above © CQ Products.

ISBN 978-1-4971-0283-5

Library of Congress Control Number: 2021945339

To learn more about the other great books from Fox Chapel Publishing, or to find a retailer near you, call toll free 800-457-9112 or visit us at *www.FoxChapelPublishing.com*.

We are always looking for talented authors. To submit an idea, please send a brief inquiry to acquisitions@foxchapelpublishing.com.

Printed in China
First printing

FOREWORD
BY GEORGIA PELLEGRINI

The best meals I've eaten have been around a campfire. In part it was the ingredients—a whole hog, smothered in molasses and draped in bacon, steaming over hot coals for a day until the meat fell from the bone, for example. But in part what made it memorable was the act of lighting that fire and cooking the way our early ancestors did, the act of tapping into our original human instincts. As life becomes ever more fast paced, we seem to drift further away from those original instincts, and it can sometimes be hard to find the way back. *Easy Campfire Cooking* is a roadmap. Full of handy how-tos, tips, and recipes, it is accessible to everyone, no matter how strapped to city life you are. It is a reminder that the simplicity of campfire cooking is satisfying not only because we are "going back," but because we are gathering together around the fire among friends.

Food is ultimately about community, about bringing people together. I would argue that the campfire is equally so. No matter the culture or geography, the campfire, like food, draws people in. The fact that we as humans learned how to combine the two is what made us more sophisticated cooks, and more sophisticated minds. We learned that by bringing food back to the tribe and feeding the community around the fire, we were elevating our place in the world. It is safe to say that combining food with fire was the very act that made us the humans we are today.

What is nice to see is that these types of "pioneer skills" are experiencing a renaissance. A renewed demand for books like this is a reflection that society is craving what is real and lasting versus what is fake and manufactured. People are looking for ways both large and small to step off the grid even just once in a while.

This desire to experience food within the outdoors is a wonderful thing because those who spend hours every year pondering and studying nature around them and discussing the events of the day around food and fire are reflecting something that is essential in human nature—it is the purest way of being human on this planet.

If you're looking for a taste of that, let this book be your guide. Happy cooking!

Georgia Pellegrini is the author of *Food Heroes: 16 Culinary Artisans Preserving Tradition*. Visit her blog at *georgiapellegrini.com*.

Welcome to Easy Campfire Cooking! This book is full of delicious and easy-to-make recipes for your next campfire. Whether you're a new camper or a seasoned outdoor veteran, you can cook up tasty fare for breakfast, main dishes, sides, and even desserts. With more than 250 recipes to choose from, you can't go wrong. Try Tropical Seafood Skewers (page 30), Honey Mustard Chicken Packets (page 52), Hash Brown Pie (page 69), Kayak Tuna Mac (page 98), Starry Night Chili (page 113), Fireside Pizza (page 125), and more! Whether your favorite way to cook over a fire is with a stick, skewers and kebabs, foil packets, pie irons, skillets, Dutch ovens, or using a grate, this book has you covered. So build the perfect fire, grab your cooking implements of choice, and get cookin' in the great outdoors!

CONTENTS

Main Dishes

Sides

Desserts

SKILLET

Breakfast

Main Dishes

Sides

Desserts

THE JOYS OF CAMPFIRE COOKING

What's not to love about cooking over a fire in the great outdoors? Whether you're miles away in the wilderness or as close as your own backyard, you can enjoy a beautiful sunny day or a gorgeous starry night while you cook and eat your meal outside. Best of all, cooking over a fire brings together family and friends to enjoy food and fun in a relaxing atmosphere.

To make your time outside even more enjoyable, be sure you have all your cooking supplies when you leave the house. If you carry everything in a basket or large tray, it makes transporting much easier. You may even want to restock the basket or tray after each outing so all you have to do the next time is grab and go.

Campfire cooking is something the whole family can enjoy and help with. Kids will learn the difference between a big bonfire and a cooking fire, and everyone will enjoy cooking their own food. When you're done cooking, add some extra firewood to make a roaring campfire for another great outdoor experience.

With a little imagination and some simple over-a-fire cooking tools, you'll be well on your way to creating a lot of outdoor fun for the whole family!

CAMPFIRE SAFETY

- Be sure it is legal to build a fire in your location.
- Use a fire pit, if available. Otherwise, build your fire on rock or dirt.
- Build your fire at least 8' from flammable objects.
- Never leave a fire unattended.
- Don't build a fire if it's windy. Sparks can cause an unintended fire.
- Extinguish the fire by dousing it with plenty of water. Be sure all the coals, embers and wood are wet and cool.
- Protect hands with leather gloves or heavy oven mitts and use long tongs to prevent burns.

TERMS

- **Tinder:** fallen pine needles, dry grass, wood shavings or tiny twigs
- **Kindling:** small dry sticks, larger than tinder
- **Firewood:** dry logs that are gathered, split and used for fuel
- **Hot coals:** chunks of burning firewood used for cooking, low or no flames
- **Embers:** glowing ash-covered coals

WHAT'S WOOD GOT TO DO WITH IT?

In a word—everything! You'll only get a nice cooking fire if you use the right kind of firewood. Use split logs since they produce the best heat and are easiest to ignite. Hard woods such as maple, walnut, oak or apple are best; they burn slowly and produce wonderful cooking coals.

BUILDING THE PERFECT COOKING FIRE

- Fill a bucket with water. Keep it near the fire to douse flare-ups.
- If there isn't a fire pit available, construct a U-shaped perimeter with large rocks.
- Pile up tinder in the cooking area; light with a match. When tinder is burning well, place kindling loosely on top, adding more as needed. Once kindling is burning nicely, carefully add split firewood, teepee-style, over the burning kindling.

- When the flames die down, white hot coals remain. Use a metal fire poker or long stick to distribute the coals for cooking, as needed.
- Never use gas or kerosene on a fire as they are dangerous and pose a serious risk of explosion!

GRATE IDEAS

Sometimes it's more convenient to cook food on a metal grate resting over a fire instead of cooking directly on hot coals. This offers more control over the cooking temperature. Place the grate higher for a lower cooking temperature or move it closer to the fire to increase the temperature.

If a grill is available, use it like a fire pit, building your fire inside the base. Place skewers of food, cooking pots or foil packs on top of the grate. Allow extra cooking time for this method.

If you don't have access to a grill grate, use a wire cooling rack or rack from your oven and prop it over a fire ring with rocks or empty soup cans. Set the rack at just the right height for the desired cooking temperatures.

DETERMINING THE TEMPERATURE OF A FIRE

A rule of thumb is to hold your hand palm-side down above the fire near the height the food will be cooked. The number of seconds you are able to hold your hand there determines how hot it is.

- 6 seconds ~ low heat (300°F)
- 5 seconds ~ medium-low heat (325°F)
- 4 seconds ~ medium heat (350°F)
- 3 seconds ~ medium-hot heat (375°F)
- 2 seconds ~ hot heat (400°F)

WHAT ELSE DO I NEED TO KNOW?

Cooking over a fire takes time. You don't want burned food. The best heat comes from those glowing embers. It's like a little oven in there, so find a nice spot without a lot of flame but with lots of red-hot heat.

Experiment with the heat. If you have your food too close to the fire, it will burn on the outside and be raw on the inside. Typically, keep larger food items a little further away from the heat so they cook more slowly and evenly.

Do the shuffle. Not a dance step, but the way to keep the heat evenly distributed around your food. Turn your food (but don't wave it around in the flames) and keep your stick consistently by the coals. If the "hot spot" dies down, simply move your food to another spot.

Words of wisdom. Be sure kids (and certain adults—you know who you are!) don't run with pointed sticks or use them to chase their siblings. Because a cooking stick gets hot, don't touch the cooking end immediately after it has been in the fire. Simple enough, but worth saying.

No matter which you prefer of the seven cooking methods presented in this book, one thing is for sure—there's nothing like cooking your own food in the great outdoors over a well-built fire.

WITH A STICK

So, what's the deal with food on a stick? Likely the way our ancestors cooked a long, long time ago, cooking over a fire—with the use of a stick—was what made sense in their day. Today it's just plain fun, and food cooked over a fire tastes delicious!

A cooking stick can be, quite simply, a stick you find outdoors. You're looking for a fresh stick that has some flexibility, but is strong enough to support the weight of your food. Look for something relatively long (3' to 4') to keep you safely away from the heat—singed eyebrows are not attractive!

Cooking with a stick can be as simple (s'mores and hot dogs) or as complex (entire meals) as you want it to be. Make sure you enjoy the experience, but branch out and try new and different things, too. Experiment and have fun! Remember, cooking in the great outdoors is more enjoyable and has more variety than you can shake a stick at.

If you're using a plain ol' stick, wash it with soap and water. Then use a pocket knife to carefully remove at least 6" of the bark at one end and trim that end to a point. Spray with nonstick cooking spray or rub a little vegetable oil over the trimmed cooking end of the stick before spearing your food. Cooking sticks can be tossed in the fire after your meal. No dirty dishes!

Wooden skewers need to be soaked in water for 30 minutes prior to each use to eliminate the chance of them going up in flames. Since wooden and metal skewers are too short to hold over the fire, spread the cooking coals in an even layer, then lay several large pieces of aluminum foil sprayed heavily with nonstick cooking spray over the coals and place the skewers on the foil to cook. This is where you'll need those tongs and gloves mentioned in Campfire Safety on page 9.

BREAKFAST 'BOBS

Ingredients
2 oranges
2 potatoes
1 green bell pepper, seeded
1 (8 oz.) can pineapple chunks, drained
1 (7 oz.) pkg. brown-and-serve sausage links
Fruit preserves, such as orange
    or pineapple, warmed

Directions
Cut each unpeeled orange into six wedges. Cut potatoes and bell peppers into 1" chunks. On a stick, alternately place an orange wedge, potato, pepper, pineapple chunk and a sausage link.

Cook over hot coals for 10 to 12 minutes or until sausages are hot and vegetables are tender, brushing with preserves and turning occasionally. Serve with remaining preserves.

BREAKFAST ON A STICK

Ingredients
1 C. biscuit baking mix
1 T. sugar
⅓ C. milk
1 egg
½ tsp. vanilla extract
1 (14 oz.) pkg. precooked
    smoked sausage ring
Warm maple syrup

Directions
In a large bowl, stir together baking mix, sugar, milk, egg and vanilla until well blended. Cut the sausage into seven equal pieces. Pierce a stick through one end of a sausage piece and out the other. Dip sausage in batter until thoroughly coated.

Cook above hot coals until golden brown and sausage is heated through.

Serve with maple syrup. Makes enough for seven sticks.

BREAKFAST IN A BAG

Ingredients
1 to 2 strips bacon
1 C. frozen hash browns, thawed
1 to 2 eggs

Directions
Lay bacon strips in the bottom of a lunch-size brown paper bag. Add hash browns and eggs. Fold over the top of bag, leaving a 3" space above the food. Insert stick through folded part of bag.

Hold stick so bag hangs 4" to 5" above hot coals and cook for 8 to 10 minutes or until eggs are cooked, watching closely so the bag doesn't catch on fire.

Fold down bag and eat directly from bag.

SAUSAGE & TOAST ON A STICK

Ingredients
1 (12 ct.) pkg. refrigerated breadsticks
1 (10 ct.) pkg. brown-and-serve sausage links

Directions
Insert a stick through the entire length of a sausage link, leaving about 1" of pointed end of stick exposed. Wrap the breadstick around the sausage link, sealing the ends of breadstick by pinching them around the stick at both ends of sausage.

Cook over embers, turning stick occasionally until breadstick is toasty brown and sausage is hot.

BACON ON A STICK

Insert a stick into one end of a strip of bacon and push onto stick about 6". Wrap bacon around stick, poking the end of the stick through the other end of the bacon. Cook above hot coals until crisp.

EGG ON A STICK

Use the tip of a skewer or sharpened stick to carefully make a small hole in each end of a whole egg. Slowly slide the sharpened stick into the hole in the wide end and out the hole in the narrow end, making sure there is about 1" of stick showing outside the narrow end.

Hold stick parallel to the ground while placing the small end of egg in the heat until some of the egg white leaks out and solidifies on the end. Cook above hot coals, turning often, until no uncooked egg white leaks from either hole. Cook about 6 to 7 minutes for a soft-cooked egg; cook a couple more minutes if you want your egg hard-cooked.

To check for doneness, hold stick and egg over a plate and use an oven mitt to tug gently on the top side of egg. If there is a little resistance, the egg is soft-cooked. When the egg is very hard to remove from stick, it's hard-cooked.

DONUT SNAKES

Ingredients
1 tube of 8 refrigerated biscuits
¼ C. butter, melted
Cinnamon and sugar mixture

Directions
Build a campfire. Unroll each biscuit and shape into a long strip. Wrap each biscuit around a long clean stick or long metal skewer. Hold sticks so biscuits are about 6" to 10" above hot coals. When biscuits are browned, push biscuits off sticks and onto a plate. Brush biscuits with melted butter and sprinkle generously with cinnamon and sugar mixture.

HONEYED FRUIT

Ingredients
½ C. honey
1 tsp. lemon juice
Assorted fruit such as pineapple, peaches or apricots (fresh, canned or dried)

Directions
In a small bowl, stir together honey and lemon juice. Cut fruit into even sized pieces and place each piece on the end of a stick. If using dried fruits like apricots, soak in water until plump. Brush fruit with honey mixture.

Cook above the coals until heated through. Serve with remaining honey mixture, if desired.

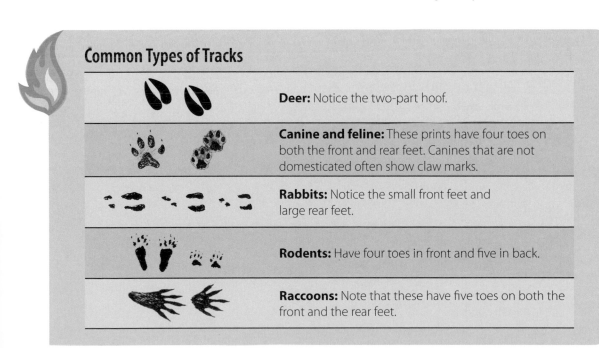

Common Types of Tracks

Deer: Notice the two-part hoof.

Canine and feline: These prints have four toes on both the front and rear feet. Canines that are not domesticated often show claw marks.

Rabbits: Notice the small front feet and large rear feet.

Rodents: Have four toes in front and five in back.

Raccoons: Note that these have five toes on both the front and the rear feet.

SIMPLE BURGERS

Ingredients
1 lb. ground beef
Salt and pepper to taste

Directions
Simply shape ground beef into about six small round or oblong patties. Insert a stick into one side and almost through the other side of each. Squeeze patty tightly around stick. Sprinkle with salt and pepper.

Cook above hot coals until patties are brown on the outside and cooked to desired doneness.

MEATBALL SUBS

Ingredients
1 lb. ground beef
½ C. dry bread crumbs
4 eggs
½ C. milk
¾ C. grated Romano cheese
1 tsp. onion salt
1 clove garlic, minced
¼ C. finely chopped fresh parsley
¼ C. finely chopped fresh basil
1 C. spaghetti sauce
4 sub buns or hot dog buns

Directions
In a large bowl, mix together ground beef, bread crumbs, eggs, milk, Romano cheese, onion salt, garlic, parsley and basil until well combined. Add more bread crumbs if the mixture is too wet; add an extra egg if it's too dry. Roll mixture into 1½" balls, and place several meatballs on the end of each stick.

Cook above hot coals until meatballs are cooked to desired doneness.

Drizzle about 1 tablespoon spaghetti sauce on each meatball and hold over the fire for a few seconds until sauce is hot.

Remove meatballs from stick and place on buns.

Quick Tip:
"When choosing a kitchen area [at your campsite], you'll want to make sure you're satisfying as many aesthetical and functional factors as possible. These factors include: a good view, comfortable lounging, easy to tarp if the weather is inclement, close to water, and not too far from the tents." (from *Canoe Camping* by Mark Scriver)

APPLE-GLAZED PORK

Ingredients

1 lb. boneless pork loin
Salt to taste
¼ C. lemon juice, divided
2 T. butter
1 C. apple jelly
1 tsp. ground cinnamon

Directions

Cut pork loin into 1" cubes. Sprinkle with salt and drizzle with 2 tablespoons lemon juice. Place pork on sticks. Melt together butter and jelly. Stir in cinnamon and remaining 2 tablespoons lemon juice. Brush glaze over pork.

Cook above hot coals for 10 to 12 minutes, turning and basting often with glaze to make a few of your friends happy campers.

BEEF ROLL-UPS

Ingredients

½ lb. flatiron steak*
Yellow or spicy brown mustard to taste
Salt and pepper to taste
Minced garlic to taste
¼ C. finely chopped onion, divided
¼ C. finely chopped fully cooked
    bacon or bacon bits, divided
4 mini dill pickles
Toothpicks
Kitchen string

* Try other cuts of beef, such as top round
   or sirloin tips, or use bacon.

Directions

Cut or pound beef to ¼" thickness. Cut into strips about as wide as the length of a pickle and long enough to just wrap around a pickle. Spread each strip with mustard, season with salt, pepper and garlic and sprinkle with about 1 teaspoon each onion and bacon. Place a pickle near one short end of each strip and roll beef tightly around pickle; secure ends with a toothpick. Use kitchen string to securely tie each pickle and beef strip together; remove toothpick. Insert a stick through one long side and out the other for each roll-up.

Cook over hot coals about 5 minutes on each side or until beef is cooked to desired doneness. Remove from stick and cut strings before serving.

CATCH OF THE DAY, THE STICK WAY

Ingredients

1 (2 to 3 lb.) fresh trout, head intact
Salt and pepper to taste

Directions

Clean and gut the fish. Season fish inside and out with salt and pepper. Push the end of the stick lengthwise through the stomach of the fish and into the head. Wearing heavy gloves or using heavy oven mitts, push the other end of the stick into the ground at an angle near the coals, positioning it so the fish hangs above the fire pit.

Position rocks around the stick to help hold it in place.

Cook over hot coals for 15 to 20 minutes or until the thickest part of the fish flakes easily, repositioning the stick during cooking as needed. If the fish begins to burn, move the stick further away from the coals.

Use gloves or oven mitts to remove the stick from the ground and set the fish (still on the stick) on a serving plate. Then remove the stick. Feeds one or more.

Quick Tip:
Try brushing cleaned fish with an olive oil and lemon juice mixture. Starting at tail end, poke a wooden skewer through the fish with the pointed end coming out through its mouth. Place fish in coals (no flames) head first with tail sticking up. Cook about 10 minutes until 165°F.

SIMPLY HOT DOGS

Ingredients
6 hot dogs
6 hot dog buns
Condiments of your choice

Basic Cooking Directions
Insert a stick into the end of each hot dog, about halfway through or into a long side, completely through. Cook above hot coals until hot dogs are cooked to your liking. Serve on a bun with condiments of your choice. Ashes should not be considered a condiment, however, so don't drop the hot dog in the fire!

MIX IT UP!

Simply Sausages: Replace hot dogs with fully cooked sausage links. Follow Basic Cooking Directions above.

Dipped Dogs: Place ketchup and finely crushed flaked corn cereal on separate plates. Roll hot dogs in ketchup and then in cereal. Follow Basic Cooking Directions above, but watch closely so the cereal doesn't burn.

Chili Dogs: Heat a can of chili. Follow Basic Cooking Directions above. Serve hot dogs covered in chili.

Bacon Cheese Dogs: Make a slit in one long side of each hot dog without cutting through. Fill each slit with a little shredded Cheddar cheese. Beginning at one end, wrap one bacon slice around each hot dog, covering hot dog completely. Follow Basic Cooking Directions above, cooking until bacon is crisp.

Dough Dogs: Wrap a slice of American cheese around each hot dog. Wrap a refrigerated biscuit around each, pinching edges to seal and making sure cheese is covered. Follow Basic Cooking Directions above, cooking for 12 to 18 minutes or until dough is golden brown, turning as needed to brown all sides.

Dogs & 'Kraut: Make a slit in one long side of each hot dog without cutting through. Fill slit with 1 tablespoon drained sauerkraut. Wrap a refrigerated biscuit around each hot dog, pinching edges to seal and making sure sauerkraut is covered completely. Follow Basic Cooking Directions above, cooking for 12 to 18 minutes or until dough is golden brown, turning as needed to brown all sides.

Frank Kebabs: Cut hot dogs and whole dill pickles into equal-sized chunks. Alternately place on a stick and follow Basic Cooking Directions above. Slide hot dog and pickle chunks together onto a bun.

HAWAIIAN ROASTS

Ingredients

Makes 4 servings
4 to 6 hot dogs, cut into pieces
1 (20 oz.) can pineapple chunks, drained

Directions

Build a campfire. Slide hot dog pieces and pineapple chunks onto 4 pointed sticks. Hold sticks about 8" to 10" above hot coals. Cook until hot dogs are heated throughout, about 5 to 8 minutes.

LITTLE WEINER KEBABS

Ingredients

Makes 4 servings
1 pkg. Hillshire Farm little smokies
4 dill pickles, cut into ¾" pieces
1 pint cherry tomatoes
1 (4 oz.) can button mushrooms, drained
15 large pimiento-stuffed green olives
1 green bell pepper, cut into ¾" squares

Directions

Build a campfire. Slide little smokies, pickle pieces, cherry tomatoes, button mushrooms, green olives and green bell pepper squares onto 4 pointed sticks. Hold sticks about 8" to 10" above hot coals. Cook until little smokies are heated throughout, about 5 to 8 minutes.

Quick Tip:

Instead of hot dogs, try substituting metts (smoked sausage), brats, Italian sausage, Polish sausage or Kielbasa. Cut sausages into bite-size pieces to ensure thorough cooking to 165°F with no pink remaining.

STICK 'TATERS

Ingredients

12 (1½") new or baby potatoes
2 C. plain yogurt
Salt, pepper and garlic salt to taste

Directions

In a small bowl, combine potatoes, yogurt, pepper and garlic salt; stirring to coat well. Marinate for 20 to 30 minutes.

Insert a stick into the center of the potatoes, threading three on each stick. Cook above the coals for about 10 minutes or until crisp-tender.

WHEAT DOUGH

Ingredients

1½ C. white flour
1 C. whole wheat flour
¼ C. bran
¼ C. wheat germ
1 T. baking powder
½ tsp. salt
⅓ C. nonfat dry milk
⅓ C. solid vegetable shortening

Directions

In a large bowl, stir together white flour, wheat flour, bran, wheat germ, baking powder, salt and dry milk. Add shortening, blending until mixture resembles coarse crumbs. Slowly add water, a little at a time, just until blended and the dough is stiff and holds together. Follow Basic Cooking Directions below.

Basic Cooking Directions

Remove a couple tablespoonfuls of dough from the bowl, knead it together and wrap it around the end of a stick. Cook above the coals for 12 to 18 minutes, rotating to cook evenly until golden brown on the outside and baked completely on the inside.

QUICK STICK BREAD

In a small bowl, stir together 1 cup biscuit baking mix and ¼ cup water until a soft dough forms. Follow Basic Cooking Directions above.

BREAD DOUGH (A.K.A. BANNOCK DOUGH)

Ingredients
2 to 3 C. flour
1 to 2 T. baking powder
1 tsp. salt, optional
2 to 3 T. vegetable oil

Directions
In a large bowl, stir together flour, baking powder, salt and oil. Mix until crumbly. Slowly add ⅔ cup warm water, a little at a time, mixing until dough feels soft. Don't add extra water; continue to work the dough until it holds together. Follow Basic Cooking Directions on page 21.

VARIATIONS & ADD-ONS

Cheese Bread: Stir ¼ cup shredded Cheddar cheese into the dry ingredients. Add remaining ingredients and follow Basic Cooking Directions on page 21.

Garlic-Cheese Bread: Stir garlic powder and Parmesan cheese into the dry ingredients to taste. Add remaining ingredients and follow Basic Cooking Directions on page 21.

Pizza Bread: Stir about ½ cup finely shredded mozzarella cheese into dry ingredients. Add remaining ingredients and follow Basic Cooking Directions on page 21. Serve with warmed pizza sauce.

Sweet Bread: Follow Basic Cooking Directions on page 21. Remove bread from the stick and spread with butter. Roll in a mixture of cinnamon and sugar or serve with maple syrup or jam.

Éclairs: Wrap refrigerated crescent rolls around stick, folding the end of the dough around the end of the stick (you want one closed end after the dough is cooked). Follow Basic Cooking Directions on page 21. Remove bread from the stick; cool. Fill éclair with vanilla pudding. Set on a plate and frost with chocolate frosting.

Quick Tip:
Simply wrap refrigerated biscuits or breadsticks around a stick and follow Basic Cooking Directions on page 21. You can also use frozen brand dough. Simply let it thaw and rise a little before using.

NO-CRUST APPLE PIE

Ingredients
1 C. sugar
1 T. ground cinnamon
4 cooking apples, such as Jonathan
   or Granny Smith

Directions
In a small bowl, stir together sugar and cinnamon; set aside.

Insert a stick through each apple, from top to bottom without piercing the bottom, until secure. Cook 2" to 3" above hot coals, turning frequently. When the apple skin becomes brown and loose, remove apple from fire.

Leaving the apple on the stick, carefully remove skin. Sprinkle evenly with cinnamon and sugar. Hold over the coals again to sear the sugar mixture onto apple.

COCONUT CREAM PIE

Ingredients
1 lb. Italian bread
1 (14 oz.) can sweetened condensed milk
1 (14 oz.) bag sweetened flaked coconut

Directions
Slice the bread into even pieces, about 1" thick; cut pieces in half if you'd like. Put condensed milk and coconut into separate pie pans or bowls. Dip both sides of bread quickly in condensed milk, then in coconut. Insert stick into bread and cook over coals until lightly browned. Watch closely as the coconut will get dark.

Quick Tip:
Fresh raw fruit that is in season makes a healthy snack or satisfying meal end. Purchase whole fruit that is not quite ripe, so that it will ripen fully during your trip.

TOASTED WACKY TAFFIES

Makes 6 servings
6 wrapped caramel squares
12 Ritz crackers

Build a campfire. Unwrap caramel squares and insert one caramel onto the end of a pointed stick. Hold stick so caramel is about 12" to 15" above hot coals. Toast caramel over campfire just until softened, being careful not to melt caramel completely. Place one caramel between two Ritz crackers to make a sandwich. Repeat with remaining ingredients.

PINEAPPLE COBBLERS

Ingredients
2 T. brown sugar
1 T. flour
½ tsp. ground nutmeg
8 fresh pineapple spears*
1 (8 ct.) tube refrigerated crescent rolls
Caramel ice cream topping
Pecans
Sweetened flaked coconut

Directions
On a small plate, stir together brown sugar, flour and nutmeg. Roll pineapple spears in sugar mixture.

Separate crescent rolls. Place a pineapple spear along the wide end of a crescent roll triangle and roll dough around spear to the point of the triangle, folding in sides to cover. Repeat with remaining spears. Insert a stick crosswise through the center of each.

Cook above embers for 12 to 18 minutes, rotating to cook evenly until dough is golden brown on the outside and done on the inside.

Cool slightly and drizzle with ice cream topping. Sprinkle with pecans and coconut.

* Cut spears slightly shorter than the wide end of crescent roll triangle.

Fun Fact:
"The modern marshmallow was developed in the early 19th century in France and Germany. Using the 'cast and mold' process, confectioners whipped, sweetened and molded the gummy sap of the mallow root into a light and fluffy taste treat. Starch moguls later speeded the process, leading toward mass production and gelatin replacing mallow root." (from *Outdoor Parents, Outdoor Kids* by Eugene Buchanan)

BASIC S'MORE FOR 2

Ingredients
1 (1.55 oz.) milk chocolate candy bar
4 graham cracker squares
2 regular marshmallows

Directions
Place half the candy bar on each of two cracker squares; set aside.

Place marshmallows on a stick. Cook above hot coals until marshmallows are golden brown.

They will be hot! Carefully remove from stick and place one marshmallow on each candy bar half. Top with remaining two cracker squares. Enjoy!

Variations for S'mores
- Try chocolate chip cookies in place of crackers.
- Replace crackers and candy with chocolate-graham cookies.

THE NO-MESS S'MORE FOR 2

Ingredients
⅔ C. mini marshmallows
1 (1.55 oz.) milk chocolate candy bar
2 (6") flour tortillas

Directions
Break the candy bar in several small pieces. Have the candy bar and marshmallows close by.

Drape each tortilla over a stick and hold above the fire just long enough to get them nice and hot (but don't let them get crispy). Place tortillas on a plate and immediately put half the marshmallows and candy pieces on each tortilla so they begin to melt; wrap up, folding in sides.

S'more Variations for S'mores
- Try chopped peanut butter cups instead of the candy bar.
- Use chocolate frosting instead of the candy bar.
- Spread some peanut butter on the tortilla before adding chocolate.
- Replace the chocolate with butterscotch or white chocolate chips.

SHAGGY MALLOWS

Ingredients
¼ C. chocolate syrup
¼ C. sweetened flaked coconut*
2 regular marshmallows

Directions
Place chocolate syrup and coconut in separate small bowls; set aside.

Place marshmallows on a stick. Cook above hot coals until golden brown. The marshmallows will be hot! Roll marshmallow in chocolate syrup to cover. Roll in coconut.

* Or try rolling in chopped peanuts or graham cracker crumbs.

MARSHMALLOW PUFFS

Ingredients
1 (8 ct.) tube large refrigerated biscuits, such as Grands
8 regular marshmallows

Directions
Separate biscuits. Flatten each biscuit and place a marshmallow in the center. Fold biscuit around marshmallow, pressing seams to seal marshmallow inside.

Insert a stick through the biscuit and marshmallow. Cook until dough is golden brown. Eight yummy desserts.

SKEWERS AND KEBABS

A skewer is a short stick used to portion out a meal of bite-sized chunks. Skewers and kebabs are a fun way for each person to make their own customized meal. Present a variety of small food pieces and have everyone poke what they like onto a skewer. This cooking method is best used over a bare or foil-covered grill grate. If you don't have a grate, these recipes are easily converted to stick cooking— simply enlarge the food pieces so they don't break when threaded onto the stick.

BUILD YOUR OWN KEBAB

You can use nearly any combination of ingredients to make a kebab; just make sure the food is cut in nearly equal sizes on each skewer and the density of the food is nearly the same. Or fill each skewer with a different type of food and cook separately. Mix and match from the ingredients shown here—or add your own—to suit your taste. Then marinate in one of the simple marinades and follow the Basic Cooking Directions for simply delicious kebabs.

Basic Cooking Directions

Cut ingredients into even-sized pieces (1" to 2"). Marinate by placing food pieces and marinade together in a zippered plastic bag. Squeeze bag to thoroughly distribute marinade. Let set in a cool place for at least 30 minutes, turning bag occasionally. Grease a double layer of heavy-duty aluminum foil and place it on a flat bed of embers*. Place desired ingredients on a skewer or stick, without crowding food. Place skewers on foil and cook slowly until cooked to desired doneness, turning often using long tongs. Avoid cooking fast-cooking food on the same skewer with longer-cooking items.

* Or set rocks around the edge of the fire to hold a rack; cook kebabs on the rack over hot coals.

Meat
- Beef steak
- Chicken thigh or breast, boneless
- Ham, fully cooked
- Lamb chop
- Pork steak
- Pork chop
- Scallops**
- Shrimp**
- Turkey
- Venison

Vegetables
- Asparagus
- Bell peppers
- Chile peppers
- Corn on the cob
- Eggplant
- Mushrooms, whole, small**
- Onions
- Pickles
- Squash
- Tomatoes, whole cherry**
- Zucchini

Fruits
- Apples
- Apricots
- Cherries, whole, pitted**
- Orange chunks, unpeeled
- Melon, honeydew, cantaloupe
- Peaches**
- Pears
- Pineapple
- Plums**

Simple Marinades***
- Beef or chicken broth
- Fruit juice
- Italian dressing, bottled
- Marinade, bottled
- Marinade mix, dry
- Red wine
- Soy sauce
- Steak sauce
- Teriyaki sauce

** These items take very little time to cook over a fire.
*** Add extra spices to marinade, if desired.

STUFFED MEATBALLS

Ingredients
18 small mushrooms (about ¾" in diameter)
2 lbs. ground beef
1 T. finely chopped fresh chives
2 tsp. salt
Dash of pepper
3 to 4 oz. blue cheese

Directions
Remove stems from mushrooms. Finely chop the stems and set aside the caps.

In a large bowl, thoroughly combine mushroom stems, ground beef, chives, salt and pepper; divide evenly into 18 patties. Stuff each mushroom cap with a bit of blue cheese and set each stuffed mushroom in the center of a patty. Cover mushrooms completely with meat mixture, tucking and pressing edges to seal.

Place three meatballs on each of six metal or soaked wooden skewers.

Cook on a greased double layer of heavy-duty aluminum foil placed on a flat bed of embers for 20 to 25 minutes or until desired doneness, turning often.

PIZZA ON A STICK

Ingredients
1 (7 oz.) pkg. brown-and-serve sausage links
1 green bell pepper, seeded
1 onion
2 C. small fresh button mushrooms
2 C. cherry tomatoes
30 slices pepperoni
1 (10 to 13 oz.) tube refrigerated pizza crust
1½ C. shredded mozzarella cheese
1¼ C. pizza sauce, warmed

Directions
Cut sausage, bell pepper and onion into 1" chunks. On 10 metal or soaked wooden skewers, alternately thread sausage, bell pepper, onion, mushrooms, tomatoes and pepperoni.

Cut dough crosswise into 1" strips. Pierce the skewer through one end of a dough strip and wrap the remainder of the strip around vegetables and meat, pinching dough around skewer at the other end. Repeat with remaining strips.

Place on a greased double layer of heavy-duty aluminum foil and set on a grate above hot coals for 10 to 20 minutes or until dough is golden brown, turning occasionally. Remove from heat, sprinkle with mozzarella cheese and serve with pizza sauce.

SMOKY CHILE PEPPER SHRIMP

Ingredients

10 large green chile peppers, seeded
20 raw jumbo shrimp, peeled,
  deveined, tails left intact
5 T. olive oil
Salt and pepper to taste

Directions

Cut the chile peppers in half lengthwise. Tuck one shrimp into each pepper half.

Place five shrimp and peppers on each of four metal or soaked wooden skewers. Set skewers in a long shallow dish. Drizzle olive oil evenly over shrimp and peppers and sprinkle with salt and pepper. Chill for 30 minutes.

Remove skewers from marinade and reserve marinade. Cook stuffed chiles on a greased double layer of heavy-duty aluminum foil placed on a flat bed of embers for 3 to 5 minutes on each side or until shrimp become opaque, basting with reserved marinade. Discard any remaining marinade before serving.

TROPICAL SEAFOOD SKEWERS

Ingredients

⅓ C. pineapple juice
¼ C. lemon juice
¼ C. orange juice
1 T. soy sauce
2 T. olive oil
2 T. brown sugar
2 tsp. orange zest
½ tsp. ground cinnamon
¼ tsp. cayenne pepper, optional
1 ripe avocado, peeled, seeded
1 C. pineapple chunks
1 lb. raw large shrimp, peeled, deveined
½ lb. large sea scallops
1 C. honeydew melon balls

Directions

In a large zippered plastic bag, combine juices, soy sauce, oil, brown sugar, orange zest, cinnamon and cayenne pepper. Close bag and squeeze to mix thoroughly. Cut avocado into 1" chunks. Add avocado, pineapple, shrimp, scallops and melon to bag. Close and chill for 4 hours.

Alternately place food pieces on skewers; reserve marinade. Cook on a greased double layer of heavy-duty aluminum foil placed on a flat bed of embers for 5 to 10 minutes or until shrimp are pink. Baste frequently with reserved marinade; discard remainder. Do not overcook. Makes enough for six seafood lovers.

HOT STRIP KEBABS

Ingredients
2 lbs. round steak*
1 medium onion
1 clove garlic
½ C. vegetable oil
¼ C. lemon juice
2 tsp. salt
2 tsp. dry mustard
2 tsp. sugar
¼ tsp. hot sauce
Cherry tomatoes

Directions
Cut steak into ¼"-thick strips. Finely chop onion and garlic. In a zippered plastic bag, combine oil, lemon juice, salt, dry mustard, sugar and hot sauce. Close bag and squeeze to blend. Add onion, garlic and steak slices. Close bag and turn to coat steak. Marinate in a cool place for 4 to 6 hours, turning bag several times.

Drain and reserve marinade. Thread beef strips accordion-style on four to six skewers alternately with tomatoes. Cook on a greased double layer of heavy-duty aluminum foil placed on a flat bed of embers for 3 to 4 minutes on each side or to desired doneness, basting frequently with reserved marinade. Discard any remaining marinade.

* When round steak is partially frozen, it can be sliced more easily.

SWEET STEAK BITES

Ingredients
2 lbs. beef stew meat
½ tsp. Greek seasoning
¼ C. soy sauce
⅓ C. dark corn syrup
1 tsp. minced garlic
½ tsp. seasoned salt

Directions
Season stew meat with Greek seasoning. In a large zippered plastic bag, combine soy sauce, corn syrup, garlic and seasoned salt. Close bag and squeeze to blend. Add beef, turning bag to coat. Marinate overnight in a cool place, turning bag occasionally.

Place beef cubes on skewers to serve six. Cook on a greased double layer of heavy-duty aluminum foil placed on a flat bed of embers until meat is cooked to desired doneness. Because of their high sugar content, these darken quickly—watch closely.

SINGAPORE CHICKEN

Ingredients

1 red onion
2 cloves garlic, minced
Zest of 1 lemon
½ C. soy sauce
1 T. peanut oil
1 T. ground turmeric
1½ tsp. brown sugar
1 tsp. ground cumin
1 tsp. ground ginger
Salt and pepper to taste
1 lb. boneless chicken breasts

Directions

Finely chop onion and place in a large zippered plastic bag. Add garlic, lemon zest, soy sauce, oil, turmeric, brown sugar, cumin, ginger, salt and pepper. Close bag and squeeze to blend. Set aside about ¼ cup marinade. Add chicken to remaining marinade, turning bag to coat. Place bag and set-aside marinade in a cool place overnight.

Remove chicken from bag and discard used marinade. Cut each chicken breast diagonally into six strips and thread each onto a skewer. Cook on a greased double layer of heavy-duty aluminum foil placed over a flat bed of embers for 5 to 8 minutes or until cooked through, basting with set-aside marinade; turn often.

TANDOORI CHICKEN

Ingredients

4 cloves garlic
2 chile peppers, seeded
1 (2") piece fresh ginger
2 T. lime juice
1 C. plain yogurt
8 boneless chicken thighs

Directions

Finely chop garlic and chile peppers. Grate ginger. In a large zippered plastic bag, combine garlic, chile peppers, ginger and lime juice. Add yogurt; close bag and squeeze to blend. Halve each chicken thigh lengthwise. Thread four chicken pieces on each of four skewers. Arrange skewers in a nonmetal dish and pour marinade over the top. Marinate in a cool place for at least 2 hours, turning occasionally.

Remove skewers from marinade and discard marinade. Cook on a greased double layer of heavy-duty aluminum foil placed on a flat bed of embers for 8 to 10 minutes or until cooked through, turning often. This will serve four.

JERK PORK & MELON

Ingredients

2 T. peanut oil
4 tsp. Jamaican jerk seasoning
1½ lbs. boneless pork tenderloin
2 small red onions
¼ honeydew melon
½ cantaloupe
1 T. honey

Directions

Pour oil into a large zippered plastic bag. Add seasoning, close bag and squeeze to mix. Cut pork into 1½" cubes and cut each onion into four lengthwise wedges; add all pieces to bag, turning to coat food. Let stand for 30 minutes.

Alternately place pork and onion on six skewers. Cook on a greased double layer of heavy-duty aluminum foil placed on a flat bed of embers for 18 to 25 minutes or until pork is cooked through and no pink remains.

Meanwhile, cut honeydew and cantaloupe into 2" cubes; place on clean skewers and add to foil during final 5 minutes of cooking time.

Remove all skewers from heat and brush with honey.

ROASTED KOREAN PORK

Ingredients

1½ lb. pork tenderloin
3 green onions
1 T. toasted sesame seeds*
1 garlic clove, crushed
½ T. grated fresh ginger
⅓ C. soy sauce
2 T. dry sherry
2 T. sesame oil
2 tsp. sugar
½ tsp. red pepper flakes

Directions

Cut pork into thin slices. Finely chop green onions. In a large zippered plastic bag, mix together onions, sesame seeds, garlic, ginger, soy sauce, sherry, oil, sugar and red pepper flakes. Add pork slices. Close bag and turn to coat pork. Let stand in a cool place for at least 30 minutes.

Drain and reserve marinade. Thread pork slices on skewers. Cook on a greased double layer of heavy-duty aluminum foil placed on a flat bed of embers for 8 to 10 minutes or until pork is cooked through, basting and turning often to put smiles on the faces of four hungry diners.

* To toast, place sesame seeds in a dry pan over medium heat until brown; cool.

GREEK-INSPIRED LAMB KEBABS

SKEWERS AND KEBABS

Ingredients

½ onion
2 tsp. minced garlic
1 tsp. dried Greek or Turkish oregano
1 tsp. dried rosemary
1 tsp. ground cumin
½ tsp. smoked paprika
¼ tsp. pepper
2 T. lemon juice
⅓ C. olive oil, plus more for brushing
1 lb. leg of lamb
1 large red onion

Directions

Very finely chop the ½ onion. In a large zippered plastic bag, combine chopped onion, garlic, oregano, rosemary, cumin, paprika, pepper, lemon juice and oil. Close bag and squeeze to mix. Trim fat from lamb, cut into 1½" cubes and add to bag. Turn bag to coat lamb. Marinate in a cool place for 4 to 8 hours.

Remove lamb from marinade; discard marinade. Rinse lamb and let stand for 15 minutes. Cut remaining onion into 1½" chunks. Alternately place onion chunks and lamb on four skewers. Cook on a greased double layer of heavy-duty aluminum foil and place on a flat bed of embers for 8 to 11 minutes or until cooked to desired doneness.

NOMADIC VENISON

Ingredients

1 lb. venison steak
½ C. soy sauce
½ C. ketchup
½ C. sugar
1 tsp. ground ginger
1 tsp. garlic powder
1 sweet red pepper
1 onion
16 whole button mushrooms
16 cherry tomatoes

Directions

Cut venison into 1½" cubes. In a large zippered plastic bag, mix together soy sauce, ketchup, sugar, ginger and garlic powder. Add venison cubes, close bag and turn to coat. Marinate in a cool place for at least 2 hours.

Cut red pepper and onion into 1½" pieces. Remove venison from bag and discard marinade. Alternately place venison, red pepper, onion, mushrooms and tomatoes on eight skewers. Cook on a greased double layer of heavy-duty aluminum foil placed on a flat bed of embers for 8 to 11 minutes or until cooked to desired doneness.

Main Dishes

TROPICAL SHRIMP SKEWERS

Makes 2 servings

¼ C. barbecue sauce
2 T. pineapple or orange juice
2 nectarines
10 oz. medium shrimp, peeled and deveined
1 yellow onion, cut into wedges

Place grilling grate over campfire. In a medium bowl, combine barbecue sauce and pineapple juice and set aside. Cut each nectarine into 6 wedges. Slide shrimp, nectarines and onion wedges onto 4 long skewers. Place skewers on hot grate and grill for 4 to 5 minutes, brushing often with the barbecue sauce mixture. Shrimp are done when they turn opaque.

COWBOY KEBABS

Makes 4 servings

½ C. spicy steak sauce
½ C. barbecue sauce
2½ tsp. prepared horseradish
1 (1½ lb.) beef top round steak,
    cut into ½" thick strips
4 medium red skin potatoes, cut into wedges
1 medium onion, cut into wedges
⅓ C. red bell pepper strips
⅓ C. green bell pepper strips
⅓ C. yellow bell pepper strips

Soak 8 (10") wooden skewers in water for 30 minutes. In a medium bowl, combine steak sauce, barbecue sauce and horseradish. In a heavy-duty ziplock bag, combine steak strips and vegetables. Pour in steak sauce mixture and seal. Let steak and vegetables marinate in a cooler filled with ice for 1 hour. Place grilling grate over campfire. Alternating, slide steak strips (like an accordion), potato wedges, onion wedges and bell pepper strips onto skewers. Place skewers on hot grate and grill for 6 to 10 minutes or until steak pieces reach desired doneness.

TERIYAKI-CHICKEN KEBABS

Makes 6 servings

4 boneless, skinless chicken breast
  halves, cut into 1" cubes
2 medium zucchini, cut into
  ½" thick slices
1 green bell pepper, cut into 1" squares
1 small red onion, cut into ½" cubes
1 C. teriyaki sauce, divided
½ tsp. Lawry's seasoned pepper
¼ tsp. garlic powder

In a heavy-duty ziplock bag, place chicken cubes, zucchini slices, green bell pepper squares and red onion cubes. Pour ¾ cup teriyaki sauce into bag and seal. Let chicken and vegetables marinate in a cooler with ice for 30 minutes. Place grilling grate over campfire. Slide marinated chicken and vegetables onto long metal skewers. Sprinkle skewers with Lawry's seasoned pepper and garlic powder. Place skewers on the hot grate and grill kebabs for 10 to 15 minutes or until chicken is cooked throughout. Baste kebabs with remaining ¼ cup teriyaki sauce, however, avoid basting during last 5 minutes of grilling time.

BEER BRAT STICKS

Makes 6 servings

5 beer bratwursts, cut into 1" pieces
1 zucchini, cut into 1" pieces
1 yellow squash, cut into 1" pieces
1 red onion, cut into 1" pieces
1 green bell pepper, cut into 1" pieces
1 red bell pepper, cut into 1" pieces
2 C. fresh button mushrooms
2 C. barbecue sauce

Place grilling grate over campfire. Soak 6 (10") wooden skewers in water for 30 minutes. Slide bratwurst pieces, zucchini pieces, squash pieces, onion pieces, bell pepper pieces and mushrooms onto skewers. Place skewers on hot grate and grill for 12 to 15 minutes, brushing often with the barbecue sauce. Grill kebabs until bratwurst pieces are cooked throughout.

"The Black Feather [Wilderness Adventures] philosophy about food on the trail is that it should be one of the highlights of the day. In the camp kitchen, the great stories of the day are recounted, jokes are told, ideas are shared and the problems of the world are solved." (from *Camp Cooking in the Wild* by Mark Scriver, Wendy Grater and Joanna Baker)

PORK & PEACH SKEWERS

Makes 4 servings

⅓ C. balsamic vinegar
3 T. olive oil
1 T. honey
2 garlic cloves, minced
1 tsp. coarse salt
1 tsp. black pepper
1 to 1½ lbs. pork tenderloin
2 or 3 fresh firm peaches
1 onion

Combine balsamic vinegar, olive oil, honey, garlic, salt and black pepper in a zippered plastic bag; seal and mix well. Cut pork tenderloin into 1" cubes and add to the bag; seal and shake it up until coated. Refrigerate four hours or overnight to marinate.

Before grilling, preheat a well-oiled grate over the fire. Cut peaches into 1" chunks and slice onion into wedges. Drain the pork, discarding the marinade. Thread meat, peaches and onion onto skewers, alternating pieces however you like. Arrange skewers on the grate and grill 4 to 5 minutes per side or until pork is cooked through (145°F). Serve immediately.

GLAZED FRANK KEBABS

Makes 6 servings

4 hot dogs
2 ears of sweet corn, shucked
1 red onion
½ red bell pepper
½ green bell pepper
Cherry tomatoes
½ C. chili sauce
3 T. brown sugar
2 T. spicy brown mustard

Slice hot dogs and sweet corn into 1" pieces; slice red onion into wedges. Cut bell peppers into 1" pieces. Alternately thread pieces of hot dog, corn, onion, bell pepper and a few cherry tomatoes on skewers and set aside.

Combine chili sauce, brown sugar and spicy brown mustard in a bowl. Set kebabs on a grate over medium-low heat; brush skewers with some of the sauce mixture. Cover food with foil and grill about 5 minutes. Continue to cook slowly until veggies are tender, rotating kebabs every 5 minutes and brushing skewers with more sauce. Serve warm.

VEGETABLE SKEWERS

Makes 4 servings

1 red or green bell pepper, cut into 1" pieces
1 zucchini, cut into ½" pieces
1 yellow squash, cut into ½" pieces
2 (6 oz.) pkgs. large mushrooms
2 T. olive oil
2 T. red wine vinegar

Place grilling grate over campfire. In a heavy-duty ziplock bag, place bell pepper pieces, zucchini pieces, yellow squash and mushrooms. Pour olive oil and red wine vinegar in bag and seal. Let vegetables marinate for 15 minutes. Slide vegetables onto four long metal skewers. Place vegetable kebabs on hot grate and grill for 5 to 10 minutes, brushing occasionally with remaining olive oil mixture. Grill until vegetables are tender and lightly browned.

TOASTY CHEESE CUBES

Ingredients

Halloumia cheese*
Olive oil
Fresh oregano

Directions

Cut cheese into 1" to 2" cubes. Place cheese cubes onto metal or soaked wooden skewers. Set the skewers in a long shallow dish. Drizzle all slices with oil and sprinkle with oregano. Set several rocks around the outside of the embers and set a grill grate on rocks. Cook cheese on grate for a few minutes until cheese starts to droop just a little, turning often (don't wait until it starts to melt or you'll have a mess).

* Halloumia cheese has a very high melting point and can stand up to the heat. It can usually be found in whole food stores, specialty markets or online. Other cheeses, such as provolone and sharp Cheddar can also be cooked for a short time before melting.

STRAWBERRY MERINGUES

Ingredients
Strawberries
Melted chocolate candy wafers
Marshmallow fluff

Directions
Dip delicious ripe strawberries in melted chocolate (you can melt it right at the fire).

Let chocolate harden, then dip in fluff.

Thread a berry onto a skewer and hold over hot coals to toast. Take care not to place directly in flames. Fluff will turn golden when done.

FOIL PACKETS HOBO-STYLE

Foil can be wrapped around food to create airtight packages to set directly on a bed of hot coals or embers. When the edges are sealed well, the pack can be flipped over during cooking and steam develops inside to cook the food. Check and rotate foil packs often to prevent overcooking in one spot, especially those containing sugar.

Even though one layer of heavy-duty foil is adequate for most foil packs, using a double (or triple) layer is ideal because it prevents punctures and keeps dirt or ashes from touching your food. Wrap the food securely in one layer of foil and then place the pack, seam side down, on a second sheet of foil; wrap again. When you remove the outer layer, the inside package is clean and becomes a perfect serving dish, making clean-up a snap!

There are several ways to fold a foil pack, and you can put all the food in one big pack to serve many or make smaller packs to hold single servings.

Cut heavy-duty foil twice the circumference of the food to be wrapped. Set food in the center of foil. Bring two opposite sides of foil together above the food and roll or fold edges several times to make narrow creases; pinch to seal well. Flatten side edges and roll or fold them together in the same way to make an airtight pack. Foil packs may be placed on hot coals immediately or stored in a cooler until the fire is hot and ready for cooking.

- Foods cooked in foil packs will not brown like traditional baking, so use sauces, seasonings and colorful vegetables to add color and wrap foil snugly against the top of food to make a flat pack. This is good for meat and fish.

- To prevent hot spots, wrap a foil pack in sheets of newspaper and then wrap in a second layer of foil.

GRANOLA-STUFFED APPLES

Ingredients
2 large apples
6 T. granola cereal*
2 tsp. brown sugar
Ground cinnamon to taste
2 tsp. butter

Directions
Cut four (12") pieces of heavy-duty aluminum foil; stack in pairs. Wash and core apples but leave 1" remaining at bottom. In a small bowl, mix granola, brown sugar and cinnamon. Stuff half of granola mixture into each apple and top with butter. Wrap each apple in two sheets of foil; seal well. Set packs on medium-hot coals and cook for 20 minutes or until almost tender. Let cool 5 to 10 minutes before eating.

* To make homemade granola before leaving home, combine 4 cups oats, ¾ cup each wheat germ and oat bran and ½ cup each sunflower seed kernels, chopped almonds, pecans and walnuts. In a saucepan over medium heat, mix ½ teaspoon salt, ¼ cup each brown sugar, maple syrup and honey, ½ cup vegetable oil and 1½ teaspoons each cinnamon and vanilla. Bring to a boil; pour over dry ingredients, stirring to coat. Spread on baking sheet and bake at 325°F for 20 minutes or until toasted, stirring after 10. Cool; stir in raisins. Store in an airtight container.

WRAPPED APPLES

Makes 2 servings
2 Granny Smith apples, cored
2 T. brown sugar
½ tsp. cinnamon

Build a campfire. Core apples and fill the core of each apple with 1 tablespoon brown sugar and ¼ teaspoon cinnamon. Wrap each apple completely in a large piece of aluminum foil, twisting the extra foil at the top to make a handle. Place wrapped apples directly in the coals of the campfire and cook for 5 to 10 minutes, until softened. Using long tongs, remove apples from fire. Using a hot pad or oven mitt, slowly unwrap apples, being careful not to spill any hot sugar. Eat apples with a fork.

Quick Tip:
To bury a foil pack in hot coals, create one with handles. After sealing the top edge, twist both ends of foil like corkscrews and bend them up to make two handles. Use tongs to remove the pack from the fire.

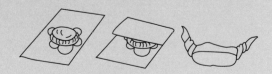

SUN'S UP HILLBILLY TRASH

Ingredients
Seasoned salt to taste, divided
2 T. butter, cut in pieces, divided
½ (24 oz.) bag shredded hash brown potatoes
4 eggs, lightly beaten
½ onion, chopped
½ (12 oz.) pkg. diced cooked ham
1 C. shredded Cheddar cheese
Salt and pepper to taste

Directions
Line a large bowl with three (18") pieces of heavy-duty aluminum foil, criss-crossing pieces, with edges extending 4" above top of bowl. Grease foil with nonstick cooking spray. Sprinkle lightly with seasoning salt and add half the butter pieces.

In a large zippered plastic bag, combine hash browns, eggs, onion, ham and cheese; carefully squeeze bag to mix well. Pour potato mixture into foil-lined bowl. Top with remaining butter pieces; sprinkle with seasoned salt, salt and pepper as desired. Seal foil edges together at the top to create a pouch, leaving room for ingredients to expand.

Remove pouch from bowl and place on medium-hot coals. Cook about 1 hour or until potatoes are tender and eggs are cooked. Open pouch carefully to stir several times during cooking and then reseal; rotate pouch as needed for even heat. Remove from fire, open pouch and use a large spoon to dish up five servings.

Variations
- Substitute ground breakfast sausage for the diced ham and add diced red or green bell pepper.

POTATOES & EGGS

Ingredients
1 baking potato per person
Butter
1 egg per person
Salt and pepper to taste

Directions
Coat the outside of scrubbed potato with butter; wrap tightly in heavy-duty aluminum foil. Place potato into hot coals for 45 to 60 minutes or until tender. Remove from heat and carefully unwrap. Slice potato partway through and open it slightly. Place some butter inside and then break an egg into potato; rewrap in foil. Return to coals, egg side up and bake until egg is set. Season with salt and pepper.

ORANGE-OATMEAL MUFFINS

Ingredients

6 large oranges
1 (7 oz.) pkg. oatmeal muffin mix
Egg and milk as directed on
    muffin mix package
2 T. butter, softened

Directions

Cut off the top ¼ of each orange. Remove pulp to make hollow shells and lids. Prepare muffin batter with egg and milk as directed on package. Lightly butter the inside of orange shells; do not butter lids. Pour muffin batter into each shell, filling ½ full. Cover with orange lids and wrap tightly in heavy-duty aluminum foil. Set on hot coals for 20 to 30 minutes or until cooked through. Remove foil and eat with a spoon. Also makes great snacking for six.

CINNAMON ROLL CUPS

Makes 4 servings

4 oranges
1 tube of 10 refrigerated biscuits
4 tsp. cinnamon
½ C. powdered sugar
4 tsp. milk

Build a campfire. Cut top ⅓ from each orange and scrape out pulp. Eat or discard pulp. Separate tube into individual biscuits. Mash biscuits into round circles. Sprinkle 4 of the biscuits with 1 teaspoon cinnamon and ½ tablespoon powdered sugar. Top biscuits with another biscuit and sprinkle with 1 teaspoon cinnamon and ½ tablespoon powdered sugar. Divide remaining 2 biscuits into 4 parts. Flatten four remaining parts and place on top of each biscuit. Roll up layered biscuits and place inside the hollowed orange peel cups. Divide remaining 4 tablespoons powdered sugar into each orange and pour 1 teaspoon milk into each orange. Replace top peel of orange and wrap each orange in aluminum foil. Place wrapped oranges directly in the coals of the campfire and cook for 30 minutes. Using long tongs, remove oranges from fire. Using a hot pad or oven mitt, slowly unwrap oranges and peel oranges to reveal cooked biscuits.

DONUT SURPRISE

Ingredients

6 cake donuts, cut in half like a bagel
Fruit pieces of choice (sliced apples,
    peaches, pineapple rings or berries)
½ C. sugar
3 T. ground cinnamon

Directions

On half of each donut, arrange pieces of fruit. Stir together sugar and cinnamon; sprinkle mixture over fruit. Replace top half of donut and wrap tightly in heavy-duty aluminum foil. Place in embers for 5 to 10 minutes or until heated through.

MAKE MINE MEATLOAF

Ingredients

2 lbs. lean ground beef
1 egg, lightly beaten
½ C. seasoned bread crumbs
½ (10.7 oz.) can tomato soup
Salt and pepper to taste

Directions

Cut one (18") piece of heavy-duty aluminum foil. Set ground beef in the center and make a well in the middle of meat. Add egg, bread crumbs, soup, salt and pepper; mix well with hands. Shape meat mixture into one large loaf*.

Wrap foil around meatloaf, leaving some room at the top for steam. Wrap in two sheets of newspaper and wrap again in another piece of foil, sealing well. Set pack on medium-hot coals for 45 minutes, moving it several times during cooking for even heat. Let stand 5 minutes before opening pack. Slice meatloaf to serve about eight hungry campers.

* For individual foil packs, let each person create their own meatloaf shape from part of meat mixture. Top with ketchup, barbeque sauce or teriyaki sauce as desired; wrap each loaf in foil. Reduce cooking time (20 to 30 minutes or until cooked through).

JUNGLE JAMBALAYA

Ingredients

1 green bell pepper, seeded and chopped
1 onion, chopped
2 boneless chicken breast halves, cubed
1 (14 oz.) pkg. kielbasa sausage, sliced
5 red new potatoes, cubed
1 (4 oz.) can tiny shrimp, optional
1 (14.5 oz.) can diced tomatoes
¾ C. quick-cooking rice
2 tsp. Cajun seasoning
¼ C. olive oil

Directions

Cut three (20") pieces of heavy-duty aluminum foil and stack two pieces together. In layers down the center of double foil, arrange bell pepper, onion, chicken, sausage, potatoes and shrimp, if desired. In a bowl, mix tomatoes, rice and Cajun seasoning. Spread tomato mixture over food on foil. Drizzle with oil and use a large spoon to lightly toss ingredients.

Bring long edges of foil together at the top and seal well; seal side edges of foil pack. Wrap remaining foil over pack and around the bottom, crimping to hold. Set pack over medium-hot coals and cook for 50 to 60 minutes or until chicken is cooked through and vegetables are tender. Turn pack over once after 30 minutes.

THREE-MINUTE PIZZA

Makes 10 servings
1 pkg. 5 Pita bread slices
1 (15 oz.) can pizza sauce
4 C. shredded mozzarella cheese
Pepperoni slices
Additional pizza toppings, optional

Build a campfire. Cut each pita bread in half to make 10 pita pockets. Spoon pizza sauce into pita pockets, spreading evenly. Add shredded mozzarella cheese, pepperoni slices and any additional toppings desired. Wrap each pita pocket in aluminum foil. Place wrapped packets directly in the coals of the campfire and cook for 3 minutes, turning once. Using long tongs, remove packets from fire. Using a hot pad or oven mitt, slowly unwrap packets.

HAWAIIAN HAM DELIGHT

Makes 1 serving
2 pieces thick-sliced ham
1 potato, peeled and cubed
2 carrots, peeled and sliced
1 (20 oz.) can crushed pineapple
1 tsp. brown sugar

Build a campfire. Place ham slices, cubed potatoes, sliced carrots, pineapple pieces and brown sugar on a large piece of aluminum foil. Sprinkle with some of the pineapple juice from can. Wrap aluminum up and over ingredients to seal the packet. Wrap packet again in aluminum foil. Place wrapped packet directly in the coals of the campfire and cook for about 20 minutes, turning after every 5 minutes. Using long tongs, remove packet from fire. Using a hot pad or oven mitt, slowly unwrap packet.

PORK CHOP PACKAGE

Makes 1 serving
1 pork chop
1 large potato, cubed
1 large carrot, peeled and sliced
1 onion, cut into wedges
Lawry's seasoning salt

Build a campfire. Place pork chop, cubed potatoes, sliced carrots and onion wedges on a large piece of aluminum foil. Sprinkle with seasoning salt to taste. Wrap aluminum up and over ingredients to seal the packet. Wrap packet again in aluminum foil. Place wrapped packet directly in the coals of the campfire and cook for 30 minutes, turning after 15 minutes. Using long tongs, remove packet from fire. Using a hot pad or oven mitt, slowly unwrap packet.

STUFFED GREEN PEPPERS

Ingredients

6 green bell peppers
1 lb. lean ground beef
1 small onion, chopped
2 C. cooked rice*
2 T. butter
¼ to ⅓ C. chili sauce
Salt to taste
Shredded Parmesan or Cheddar cheese

Directions

Cut the tops off the peppers and remove seeds. In a bowl, combine ground beef, onion, rice, butter, chili sauce and salt. Stuff each pepper shell with a portion of beef mixture.

Wrap each stuffed pepper in a double layer of heavy-duty aluminum foil. Set packs in medium-hot coals and cook for 25 to 35 minutes, rotating occasionally, until meat is cooked through and a themometer inserted in the center reads 160°F. Remove from fire, open packs and sprinkle with cheese before serving.

* Prepare rice before you leave on your trip and store in an airtight container; chill until needed. Or, to cook rice over your campfire, use a foil pot and bring 1 cup water to a boil. Add 1 cup instant rice and cover pot with foil; let stand for 5 minutes or until all water is absorbed.

SPAM PACKS

Makes 2 servings

1 (12 oz.) can Spam, cut ¼" thick
1 (20 oz.) can crushed pineapple, drained
1 (15 oz.) can yams, drained
1 (15 oz.) can whole white potatoes, drained
2 T. butter
1 C. dark brown sugar

Build a campfire. Set out two large pieces of aluminum foil. Divide Spam slices, drained pineapple, drained yams and drained white potatoes onto aluminum foil pieces. Place 1 tablespoon butter on top of ingredients in each packet. Sprinkle brown sugar evenly over ingredients in packets. Wrap aluminum up and over ingredients to seal the packets. Wrap packets again in aluminum foil. Place wrapped packets directly in the coals of the campfire and cook for 20 minutes, turning once. Using long tongs, remove packets from fire. Using a hot pad or oven mitt, slowly unwrap packets.

Quick Tip:

"Keep the eating and kitchen utensils [at the campsite] in a nylon apron with different pockets to keep them organized and handy." (from *Canoe Camping* by Mark Scriver)

HAM & SWEET POTATOES

Ingredients

- 1 (8 oz.) pkg. fully cooked diced ham
- 1 (15 oz.) can sweet potatoes, cubed, juice reserved
- 1 (8 oz.) can pineapple chunks, drained
- ½ C. butter, divided
- ¼ C. brown sugar, divided

Directions

Cut four (15") pieces of heavy-duty foil. On the center of each foil piece, layer ¼ each of the ham, sweet potatoes and pineapple. Put 2 tablespoons butter and 1 tablespoon brown sugar on top of each serving. If desired, drizzle a spoonful of reserved sweet potato juice over the top.

Wrap foil around food, sealing well. Set foil packs on embers (or on a grate over a medium-hot fire) and cook for 20 minutes, turning packs over halfway through cooking. Serves four hungry guests.

STUFFED ONIONS

Ingredients

- 4 extra-large sweet onions
- 1 lb. thinly sliced pork sirloin steak, chopped
- 2 tsp. salt
- Pepper to taste
- ½ tsp. ground cumin
- 1 C. dry cornbread stuffing mix
- 1 T. chili powder, or more to taste
- 3 T. diced green chiles, drained
- 1 (15.5 oz.) can hominy, drained
- ¼ C. chopped red or green bell pepper
- ½ C. grated Parmesan cheese

Directions

Slice the top ¼ off each onion. Slice off bottoms so onions set flat; peel off papery skins. Cut an "X" in the center of each onion and scoop out center portion, leaving ½"-thick walls. Dice ¼ cup of removed onion to use in filling. In a bowl, mix diced onion, steak, salt, pepper, cumin, stuffing mix, chili powder, chiles, hominy, bell pepper and cheese. Fill each onion bowl with a portion of mixture.

Cut four large pieces of heavy-duty foil. Wrap foil around each upright stuffed onion, sealing well and flattening top slightly. Set onions in hot coals, placing one or two hot coals on top of each pack. Cook for 30 minutes or until a meat thermometer inserted in the center reaches 175°F. Remove from coals and open carefully.

SPINACH-MUSHROOM CHEESEBURGERS

Ingredients

½ onion, sliced and separated into rings
1 (10 oz.) pkg. frozen chopped
   spinach, thawed
2 lbs. lean ground beef
1 (1 oz.) pkg. dry onion soup mix
1 C. chopped mushrooms
Salt and pepper to taste
1 C. shredded mozzarella cheese, divided
6 to 8 hamburger buns, optional

Directions

Cut six to eight (15") pieces of heavy-duty aluminum foil. Place several onion rings on the center of each foil piece and set aside. Squeeze liquid from spinach and break apart into a bowl. Add ground beef, soup mix, mushrooms, salt and pepper; mix well. Divide meat mixture evenly and shape into 6 to 8 patties. Set one patty on top of onions on each foil piece.

Wrap foil around food and seal well. Place packs on hot coals for 7 to 10 minutes; turn packs over and cook for 7 to 10 minutes longer or until meat is cooked through. Carefully open packs and sprinkle patties with cheese. When melted, serve on buns with desired condiments.

TURKEY & STUFFING POUCHES

Ingredients

Butter
1 (6 oz.) pkg. instant stuffing mix, prepared*
1 fully cooked boneless turkey breast, sliced
4 carrots, thinly sliced
½ tsp. chicken bouillon mixed with
   ⅓ C. water

Directions

Cut four to six (18") pieces of heavy-duty aluminum foil. Fold up edges to contain liquid. Place a pat of butter on each piece of foil topped with about ½ cup prepared stuffing. Arrange one or two turkey slices on stuffing and divide remaining stuffing among packets. Dot with another pat of butter; set some carrots on top. Drizzle bouillon water evenly over each packet.

Wrap foil tightly around food, sealing well. Set foil packs in medium-hot coals and cook for 30 to 45 minutes, rotating frequently until carrots are tender and food is hot. Serves four to six thankful people.

* Follow package directions to prepare stuffing; store in an airtight container in a cooler until needed.

FOIL PACKETS HOBO-STYLE

Main Dishes

SWEET & SOUR CHICKEN

Ingredients

¼ C. ketchup
2 T. apple cider vinegar
2 T. brown sugar
1 (8 oz.) can pineapple chunks, drained
1 green bell pepper, chopped
1 onion, chopped
4 boneless chicken breast halves
Salt and pepper to taste

Directions

Before leaving home, prepare the sweet and sour sauce. In a medium saucepan, combine ketchup, vinegar, brown sugar, pineapple chunks, bell pepper and onion. Bring to a low simmer, stirring occasionally. Let cool and pour into an airtight storage container; refrigerate. Transport sauce in your cooler.

To prepare chicken, cut four (15" to 18") pieces of heavy-duty aluminum foil and fold up the edges to contain sauce. Spoon a portion of prepared sweet and sour sauce onto each foil piece. Set a chicken piece on top and spoon more sauce over each one. Season with salt and pepper. Wrap foil around chicken, sealing well. Set foil packs on medium-hot coals for 30 to 40 minutes or until chicken is cooked through. Rotate packs several times during cooking.

CHICKEN & RICE

Ingredients

4 boneless chicken breast halves
1 (10.7 oz.) can cream of chicken soup
⅔ C. uncooked instant rice
Paprika to taste
Salt and pepper to taste

Directions

Cut four (15") pieces of heavy-duty aluminum foil and grease lightly with nonstick cooking spray. Set a chicken breast half on each piece of foil. In a bowl, mix soup and rice; spoon mixture over chicken and sprinkle with paprika, salt and pepper. Wrap foil around chicken and rice, sealing well. Set foil packs on hot coals for 30 to 40 minutes or until chicken is cooked through. Rotate packs and turn several times during cooking. Dish out one pack per person.

LEMON CHICKEN

Ingredients

1 whole chicken
¼ C. melted butter
1 lemon
Seasoned salt
Lemon herb seasoning mix
½ onion, sliced

Directions

Thoroughly rinse chicken in cool water; pat dry. Cut two pieces of heavy-duty aluminum foil, large enough to wrap around the chicken; stack together. Set chicken in the center of foil. Brush with melted butter. Cut lemon in half and squeeze juice over chicken; reserve peel and pulp. Sprinkle chicken with seasoned salt and lemon herb seasoning. Place onion slices and reserved lemon peel and pulp inside chicken cavity. Wrap chicken in foil, sealing well. If desired, place chicken upside down on a third layer of foil and wrap again. Place pack on medium-hot coals and cook for 40 to 60 minutes or until cooked through. Rotate chicken several times and turn over halfway through cooking time. Let stand 10 minutes before opening foil to serve.

FAJITAS IN FOIL

Ingredients

½ (1.3 oz.) pkg. fajita seasoning mix
1½ lbs. boneless chicken
    breasts, thinly sliced
1 green or red bell pepper, seeded and sliced
1 onion, sliced
6 (6" to 8") flour tortillas

Directions

Cut six (12" to 18") pieces of heavy-duty aluminum foil and spray with nonstick cooking spray. Fold up all edges on foil to contain juice; set aside. In a large bowl, prepare fajita seasoning mix according to package directions. Add chicken, bell pepper and onion; stir until well coated. Spoon an even portion of chicken mixture and fajita sauce onto the center of each foil piece. Wrap foil around food and seal seams well to prevent leaking. Double-wrap, if desired.

Place foil packs on medium-hot embers and cook for 20 to 30 minutes, turning packs several times, until chicken is cooked through and vegetables are tender. Wrap tortillas in foil; set over warm coals during the last few minutes of cooking until warmed. Serve the contents of one foil pack with each tortilla, roll up and enjoy.

* To shorten cooking time, use precooked chicken.

SILVER GARLIC CHICKEN

Makes 2 servings

1 large skinless boneless chicken breast
½ tsp. minced garlic
1 small onion, sliced
1 medium green bell pepper, sliced
Pinch of oregano
Pinch of curry powder

Build a campfire. Place chicken breast, minced garlic, sliced onions and sliced green bell peppers on a large piece of aluminum foil. Sprinkle with oregano and curry powder. Wrap aluminum up and over ingredients to seal the packet. Wrap packet again in aluminum foil. Place wrapped packet directly in the coals of the campfire and cook for about 20 minutes, turning after every 5 minutes. Using long tongs, remove packet from fire. Using a hot pad or oven mitt, slowly unwrap packet.

ORIENTAL CHICKEN

Makes 1 serving

1 skinless boneless chicken breast
1 C. frozen mixed vegetables
2 tsp. soy sauce
Pinch of garlic salt
Pinch of cayenne pepper, optional
1 T. brown sugar

Build a campfire. Place chicken breast and frozen mixed vegetables on a large piece of aluminum foil. Sprinkle with soy sauce, garlic salt, cayenne pepper and brown sugar. Wrap aluminum up and over ingredients to seal the packet. Wrap packet again in aluminum foil. Place wrapped packet directly in the coals of the campfire and cook for about 20 to 30 minutes, until chicken is cooked throughout. Using long tongs, remove packet from fire. Using a hot pad or oven mitt, slowly unwrap packet.

FOIL-WRAPPED APRICOT CHICKEN

Makes 4 servings

4 skinless boneless chicken breasts
1 to 2 tsp. paprika
Salt and pepper to taste
4 T. apricot preserves
2 T. Dijon mustard

Build a campfire. Set out four large pieces of aluminum foil. Divide chicken breasts onto aluminum foil pieces. Sprinkle paprika, salt and pepper evenly over chicken breasts. Spoon apricot preserves and Dijon mustard evenly onto each chicken breast. Wrap aluminum up and over ingredients to seal the packets. Wrap packets again in aluminum foil. Place wrapped packets directly in the coals of the campfire and cook for 20 to 30 minutes, until chicken is cooked throughout. Using long tongs, remove packets from fire. Using a hot pad or oven mitt, slowly unwrap packets.

HONEY MUSTARD CHICKEN PACKETS

Makes 4 servings

4 skinless boneless chicken breasts
4 potatoes, quartered lengthwise
1 green or red bell pepper, cut into strips
8 to 12 T. honey mustard barbecue sauce

Build a campfire. Set out four large pieces of aluminum foil. Divide chicken breasts, potatoes and bell pepper strips onto aluminum foil pieces. Drizzle 2 to 3 tablespoons honey mustard barbecue sauce over each packet. Wrap aluminum up and over ingredients to seal the packets. Wrap packets again in aluminum foil. Place wrapped packets directly in the coals of the campfire and cook for 20 to 30 minutes, until chicken is cooked throughout. Using long tongs, remove packets from fire. Using a hot pad or oven mitt, slowly unwrap packets.

Know Your Knots

Whether you're camping or just whittling away, a good grasp of some basic knots will help you on your way. Below are three common types.

Bowline: Can be used whenever a fixed loop is needed at the end of a rope. Great for backpacking and rockclimbing; also useful to hang and hoist objects.

Clove Hitch: The best way to tie a rope to a post or ring. Great for tent pegs and securing an animal to a fence. Also the ideal knot to use when lashing objects together.

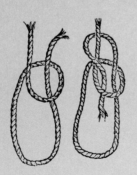

Square: Used to tie two lines together.

EASY RANCH CHICKEN

Makes 6 servings

1 (.4 oz.) env. Ranch dressing mix
¾ C. corn flakes, crushed
¾ C. grated Parmesan cheese
6 skinless boneless chicken breast halves
¼ C. butter, melted
1 red bell pepper, cut into strips

Build a campfire. Set out six large pieces of aluminum foil. In a medium bowl combine Ranch dressing mix, crushed corn flakes and Parmesan cheese. Dip chicken breast halves into melted butter and roll in crushed corn flakes mixture. Set one chicken breast half on each piece of aluminum foil and top with some of the red bell pepper strips. Wrap aluminum up and over ingredients to seal the packets. Wrap packets again in aluminum foil. Place wrapped packets directly in the coals of the campfire and cook for 20 to 30 minutes, until chicken is cooked throughout. Using long tongs, remove packets from fire. Using a hot pad or oven mitt, slowly unwrap packets.

HOT BAKED FISH

Makes 2 servings

2 trout, salmon, flounder or
    red snapper filets
1 T. olive oil
2 T. white wine, optional
Juice of ½ lemon
Salt and pepper to taste
Fresh chopped dill

Build a campfire. Place fish filets onto a large piece of aluminum foil. Sprinkle olive oil, white wine and lemon juice over fish. Season with salt, pepper and fresh chopped dill to taste. Wrap aluminum up and over ingredients to seal the packet. Wrap packet again in aluminum foil. Place wrapped packet directly in the coals of the campfire and cook for about 30 minutes. Using long tongs, remove packet from fire. Using a hot pad or oven mitt, slowly unwrap packet.

SHRIMP PACKETS

Ingredients
1 lb. shrimp, peeled and deveined
¼ C. butter or margarine, cut into pieces
1 clove garlic, minced
½ tsp. pepper
1 tsp. salt
1 C. parsley flakes

Build a campfire. Lay shrimp on a large piece of aluminum foil. Top with butter pieces, minced garlic, pepper, salt and parsley flakes. Wrap aluminum up and over ingredients to seal the packet. Wrap packet again in aluminum foil. Place wrapped packet directly in the coals of the campfire and cook for 10 to 15 minutes, until shrimp is fully cooked. Using long tongs, remove packets from fire. Using a hot pad or oven mitt, slowly unwrap packets.

Variation: Try using lemon, rosemary and red pepper flakes in place of garlic and parsley.

CHILI DOGS

Ingredients
8 hot dogs
8 hot dog buns, buttered
1 (15 oz.) can chili with or without beans
1 C. crushed corn chips
Ketchup and mustard, optional

Directions
Cut a lengthwise slit in each hot dog and place in bun. Stir together chili and corn chips. Open slit in each hot dog and spoon some of the chili mixture over hot dogs in buns.

Wrap each bun in heavy-duty aluminum foil, sealing ends well. Place packs in hot coals for 10 minutes or until heated through. Serve with ketchup and mustard, if desired. Serve one or two dogs per person.

Main Dishes

TEX-MEX FOIL PACKS

Ingredients

1 (15 oz.) can whole kernel corn, drained
2 C. cooked rice*
1 lb. fully cooked chicken strips
1 (15 oz.) can black beans
¾ to 1 C. chunky tomato salsa
1 C. shredded Cheddar cheese
¼ C. salsa verde (green salsa), optional

Directions

Cut four (15") squares of heavy-duty aluminum foil; set aside. In a large bowl, stir together corn, rice, chicken, beans (with liquid), salsa and cheese. Blend in salsa verde, if desired. Spoon an even portion of the mixture onto each piece of foil; wrap foil around food and seal well to make four airtight packs. Place packs on hot coals for 15 to 20 minutes or until heated through. Serve one pack to each person.

* Prepare rice before you leave on your trip and store in an airtight container; chill until needed. Or, to cook rice over your campfire, use a foil pot and bring 1 cup water to a boil. Add 1 cup instant rice and cover pot with foil; let stand for 5 minutes or until all water is absorbed.

FISH PACK FOR ONE

Ingredients

1 fish fillet (such as trout or perch)
½ lemon, sliced
2 to 4 cherry tomatoes, halved
Garlic salt
Lemon-pepper seasoning
⅓ C. lemon-lime soda

Directions

Cut one (15" to 18") piece of heavy-duty aluminum foil and grease lightly with nonstick cooking spray; fold up sides to create a pouch to contain liquids. Set 2 lemon slices on the center of foil and place fish on top. Sprinkle with garlic salt and lemon-pepper seasoning. Arrange tomatoes and remaining lemon slices over fish. Pour soda over fish. Wrap foil around food, sealing well. Set foil pack on hot coals for 10 to 15 minutes or until fish flakes easily. Rotate pack several times during cooking.

BASIC HAMBURGER FOIL PACK

Ingredients

1 onion slice
1 hamburger patty
1 small potato, thinly sliced
1 carrot, sliced
1 T. butter
Salt, pepper and garlic or
  seasoned salt to taste

Directions

Cut two (15") pieces of heavy-duty aluminum foil; grease lightly with nonstick cooking spray. Place onion on the center of one foil piece and top with hamburger patty, potato and carrot slices and butter. Sprinkle with salt, pepper and garlic or seasoned salt. Wrap in foil, sealing well. Wrap second piece of foil around pack in opposite direction. Place pack on hot coals and cook about 30 minutes or until meat is cooked to desired doneness and vegetables are tender. Rotate and turn pack over partway through cooking.

Try these other combos:

- Use ground turkey or sausage instead of ground beef.
- Roll hamburger into ping-pong sized balls and put two balls in each foil pack along with vegetables, mushrooms and 2 tablespoons beef gravy.
- Use canned baked beans instead of carrots.
- Use frozen hash browns instead of sliced potatoes. If unthawed, increase cooking time.
- Mix some dry onion soup mix or taco seasoning into the ground beef before shaping the patty.
- Drizzle Worcestershire, teriyaki or Tabasco sauce over the food before sealing pack.
- Sprinkle dry beef bouillon granules over food instead of salt and pepper.
- Use other vegetables instead of carrots, such as small pieces of corn on the cob, broccoli, green beans, tomatoes or peas.
- Use other seasonings and herbs such as Mrs. Dash, grill blends, onion powder, garlic cloves and bay leaves.
- Add fresh or canned (drained) mushrooms to the pack with a little extra butter.

Quick Tip:

To create extra steam inside a foil pack, add one or two ice cubes before wrapping. Placing broth, butter or high-water foods, such as onions, tomatoes and cabbage leaves inside the pack will also add moisture.

BASIC CHICKEN HOBO PACK

Ingredients

2 onion slices
1 small potato, thinly sliced
1 carrot, sliced
1 T. butter, cut into pieces
1 boneless chicken breast half
½ C. whole kernel corn, drained

Salt and pepper to taste

Directions

Cut two (18") pieces of heavy-duty aluminum foil; grease lightly with nonstick cooking spray. Arrange onion slices on the center of one foil piece. Top with potato and carrot slices and

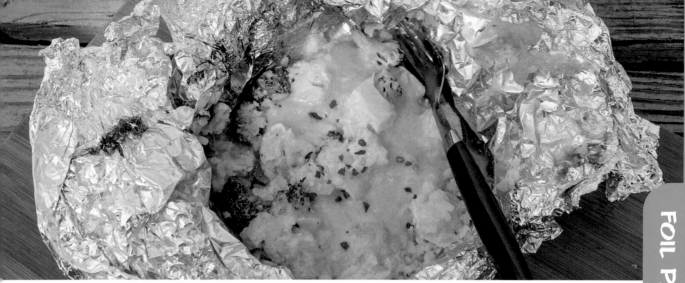

butter. Set chicken on vegetables and spoon corn over and around it. Season with salt and pepper.

Wrap in foil, allowing space at the top for steam; seal well. Wrap remaining piece of foil around pack in opposite direction. Place pack on hot coals about 30 minutes or until chicken is fully cooked and vegetables are tender. Rotate and turn pack over partway through cooking.

Try these other combos:

- Use sliced kielbasa instead of chicken.
- Use a pork chop and apple slices in place of chicken, carrots and corn.
- Try a piece of fish and lemon slices instead of chicken and onion.

- Make a pack with peeled shrimp or scallops in place of chicken; use snow peas, red bell pepper strips and sliced mushrooms in place of potatoes and corn.
- Add Italian dressing to the packet or marinate the chicken in it before assembly.
- Add cream of chicken or cream of mushroom soup to the pack.
- Stir together cream of celery soup and instant rice and use it in place of corn.
- Sprinkle granules of dry chicken bouillon or lemon pepper over the food instead of salt and pepper.
- Use a pineapple slice and sliced green bell peppers instead of potatoes and corn.
- Add lemon slices and fresh basil leaves in place of corn.
- Substitute packaged seasoning mixes, such as taco or Cajun seasoning, for the salt and pepper.
- Try other vegetables such as diced zucchini, squash and broccoli.
- Use frozen Oriental mixed vegetables, water chestnuts and baby corn in place of potatoes, carrots and corn kernels. Increase cooking time if vegetables are not thawed before use.

HAM & POTATO STUFFED PEPPERS

Ingredients
Bell peppers, any color
Frozen Southern-style hash
   browns, partially thawed
Salt and black pepper to taste
Green onions, sliced
2 T. Cheddar cheese soup
Diced ham
Eggs
Shredded Romano cheese

Directions
Cut tops off peppers. Discard seeds and ribs, but keep stem ends for "lids."

Layer some hash browns, salt, pepper, onion, soup and ham in each pepper. Stir and add a little more soup. Pour one beaten egg into each shell and cover with lid. Wrap loosely in a double layer of heavy-duty foil, sealing well on top. Set upright in hot coals for 30 to 40 minutes or until egg is cooked. Uncover and sprinkle with more onion and some cheese.

PHILLY CHEESESTEAK ON FRENCH BREAD

Makes 6 servings
Green bell peppers, sliced
Onion, sliced
¼ C. butter
1½ tsp. garlic powder
French bread loaf
Deli sliced roast beef
Provolone cheese slices

In a skillet on a grate over the fire, sauté peppers and onion in butter and garlic powder until tender. Slice bread (not all the way through) and butter both sides of slices. Cut beef and cheese into strips. Layer pepper combo, beef and cheese into each cut (the more the merrier).

Wrap loaf in heavy-duty foil and set in hot embers until cheese melts, about 20 minutes, rotating several times. Serve with veggie sticks and dip.

TOMATO & CHICKEN TORTELLINI

Makes 2 servings

2 boneless, skinless chicken breast halves
½ tsp. dried Italian seasoning
1 (9 oz.) pkg. frozen cheese tortellini, thawed
1 (14.5 oz.) can diced tomatoes with basil, garlic, and oregano, undrained
¼ C. sliced ripe olives

Cut two pieces of heavy-duty foil, each large enough to wrap around one chicken breast half with tortellini. Spray the foil pieces with nonstick vegetable spray. Place one chicken breast on each piece of foil. Sprinkle Italian seasoning on top.

Arrange half of the tortellini around each piece of chicken and top with half of the diced tomatoes. Sprinkle half of the ripe olive slices on top of the tomatoes. Wrap foil in a tent pack around each serving.

Place double-wrapped foil packs on medium-hot embers and cook for 18 to 25 minutes or until chicken is fully cooked. Move packs as needed during cooking to obtain even heating.

BRATS WITH SEASONED SAUERKRAUT

Makes 4 servings

⅓ C. green bell pepper, chopped
¼ C. onion, chopped
1½ T. brown sugar
1 tsp. yellow mustard
½ tsp. caraway seed
¾ C. sauerkraut, drained
4 fully cooked bratwursts
4 hoagie buns or large hot dog buns

In a medium bowl, combine the green pepper and onion. Stir in the brown sugar, mustard, caraway seeds and sauerkraut. Mix well. Cut two (16") pieces of heavy-duty foil. Stack foil pieces together. Spray top layer with nonstick vegetable spray. Spoon the seasoned sauerkraut in the center of the foil. Grill the brats by themselves over medium-hot coals using direct heat on a grill or long campfire forks. Turn brats several times during cooking. Place double-wrapped pack of sauerkraut on warm embers for 15 to 20 minutes or until heated through. After cooking, place one brat on each bun and spoon sauerkraut on top.

WRAPPED TUNA MELTS

Makes 4 servings

1 (12 oz.) can tuna in water, drained
2 C. cooked rice
1 C. frozen green peas
½ C. mayonnaise
1 T. lemon pepper
1½ C. shredded Cheddar cheese, divided
4 (10") flour tortillas, warmed

Cut four (16") pieces of heavy-duty foil. In a medium bowl, combine drained tuna, cooked rice, peas, mayonnaise, lemon pepper and 1 cup cheese; mix well. Spread an equal portion of tuna mixture across the center of each warm tortilla. Fold and roll up tortillas, enclosing the filling like a burrito. Place each rolled tortilla on a piece of foil with seam side down.

Wrap foil around each tortilla in a flat pack. Place double-wrapped foil packs on medium-hot embers and cook for 8 to 10 minutes. Turn packs over once during cooking. After cooking, sprinkle remaining shredded cheese on top of tortillas.

BACON-WRAPPED CABBAGE

Ingredients
1 head green cabbage
4 strips bacon
¼ C. butter
Salt and pepper to taste

Directions
Cut four (15") pieces of heavy-duty aluminum foil. Wash cabbage and cut in half; cut each half in two even wedges. Wrap a strip of bacon around each wedge and set on a piece of foil. Add about 1 tablespoon butter to each pack; season with salt and pepper.

Wrap foil around cabbage and seal tightly. Place on medium coals for 45 to 50 minutes or until cabbage is tender and bacon is cooked. Rotate and flip packs several times during cooking. Serve one pack to each person.

HERBED SNOW PEAS

Ingredients
2 C. snow peas
2 T. butter, cut into pieces
10 fresh mint leaves*, torn
Salt to taste, optional

* Try other fresh herbs such as basil, oregano or rosemary.

Directions
Place a grate over medium coals. Wash snow pea pods and lightly pat dry. Cut two (14") pieces of heavy-duty aluminum foil and stack them together. Grease lightly with nonstick cooking spray. Arrange pods on center of foil and place mint leaves over pods. Scatter butter pieces on top.

Wrap foil around food, sealing well. Place pack on the grate and cook for 15 to 20 minutes, turning halfway through cooking, until pods are crisp-tender. Divide among four diners.

CAMPFIRE VIDALIAS

Makes 4 servings
4 Vidalia onions
4 T. butter or margarine
4 cloves garlic, minced
Salt to taste

Build a campfire. Peel the outer skin from each onion and cut each onion into quarters, keeping each onion together. Place 1 tablespoon butter and ¼ of the minced garlic in the center of each onion. Wrap each onion in a double layer of aluminum foil. Place wrapped onions directly in the coals of the campfire and cook for 30 to 40 minutes. Using long tongs, remove onions from fire. Using a hot pad or oven mitt, slowly unwrap onions and season with salt to taste.

CHEESY COBS

Ingredients
5 ears fresh corn
½ C. mayonnaise
1 C. shredded Parmesan cheese
Chili powder to taste
Salt and pepper to taste

Directions
Remove husks and wash corn. Place a grate over hot coals. Brush a thin layer of mayonnaise on each ear of corn. Sprinkle ears with cheese, turning to coat all sides. Sprinkle lightly with chili powder, salt and pepper.

Wrap each ear in heavy-duty aluminum foil, sealing well; set on grate and cook for 10 to 20 minutes, turning occasionally, until kernels begin to brown.

Variation
Hobo Roasted Corn: Carefully pull back husks partway, clean off the silk and rinse ears; salt lightly, if desired. Replace husk to cover kernels. Place ears on a bed of hot coals and cook for 12 to 20 minutes or until tender, rotating ears a quarter turn every 3 to 5 minutes. Peel off the husk and spread kernels with butter.

GRILLED SQUASH

Ingredients
1 acorn or butternut squash
2 T. butter
2 T. brown sugar
Salt and pepper to taste, optional

Directions
Cut two (12" to 15") pieces of heavy-duty aluminum foil. With a sharp knife, cut squash in half lengthwise and set each half on a piece of foil. Poke a fork into the flesh inside several times; do not pierce skin. In each half, place 1 tablespoon butter and 1 tablespoon brown sugar. Season with salt and pepper, if desired.

Wrap foil around squash, sealing well. Place on medium-hot coals and cook for 45 to 60 minutes or until tender, rotating packs several times during cooking.

TOMATO & MUSHROOM POUCH

Makes 2 to 4 servings

3 to 4 large tomatoes, cut into wedges
1 (8 oz.) pkg. whole mushrooms, cleaned
    and cut in half
1 large onion, cut into wedges
½ (16 oz.) bottle French or
    Italian salad dressing
Salt and pepper to taste

Build a campfire. Place tomato wedges, mushrooms and onion wedges on a large piece of aluminum foil. Pour salad dressing over vegetables and season with salt and pepper to taste. Wrap aluminum up and over vegetables to seal the packet. Wrap packet again in aluminum foil. Place wrapped packet directly in the coals of the campfire and cook for 20 to 25 minutes. Using long tongs, remove packet from fire. Using a hot pad or oven mitt, slowly unwrap packet.

STUFFED 'TATER

Ingredients

1 small to medium potato
1 small precooked sausage
Shredded cheese
Sliced green onions

Directions

Wash potato and cut out the center with an apple corer. Insert sausage in hole. Wrap in heavy-duty aluminum foil. Place pack in medium-hot coals and cook for 45 to 60 minutes or until tender, turning often. Remove foil, slice potato and top with cheese and onions as desired.

Variations

Simple Baked Potato: Wash and poke skin of one large baking potato per person; wrap in heavy-duty aluminum foil. Cook as directed and serve with butter, sour cream, salt, pepper, bacon bits and cheese as desired.

Onion-Stuffed Potato: Wash and slice potato crosswise, at ½" intervals, without cutting through bottom. Place an onion slice between each potato slice and wrap tightly in foil. Cook as directed and serve with butter, sour cream and desired seasonings

SMOKY HOBO MUSHROOMS

Makes 6 servings

2 (10 oz.) pkgs. frozen spinach,
    thawed and well drained
¼ C. sour cream
½ C. shredded Parmesan cheese
1 tsp. garlic salt
6 portobellini mushrooms (mini portabellas)
⅓ C. shredded smoked Gouda cheese
½ C. Canadian bacon, diced

Create six stacks of double layer 12" x 18" pieces of heavy-duty foil. Line each stack with parchment paper. In a bowl, mix spinach, sour cream, Parmesan cheese and garlic salt. Set one large portobellini mushroom in the middle of each foil stack; divide the spinach mixture evenly among the mushrooms.

Divide Gouda cheese and Canadian bacon evenly over the spinach. Wrap the foil around the food and seal the edges. Set the packs directly in glowing ash for 15 minutes or until everything is hot and melty, rotating and checking every 5 minutes. Open packs carefully; season as desired.

FOIL PACKETS HOBO-STYLE

Sides

RED ONION ROAST

Ingredients

2 large red onions, skins on
2 T. vegetable oil
3 T. cream cheese, softened
1½ tsp. chopped chives

Directions

Cut four (12") pieces of heavy-duty aluminum foil and stack two pieces together; set aside. Set a grate over medium-hot coals. Brush each unpeeled onion with 1 tablespoon oil. Place each onion on a double layer of foil and wrap securely, sealing well. In a small bowl, stir together cream cheese and chives; cover and chill.

Place foil packets on the grate and cook for 45 minutes or until onions are tender. Turn packets several times during cooking. To serve, remove onions from foil, place on a serving plate and cut in half. Top each onion half with a portion of the cream cheese mixture to serve four.

SLOW-ROASTED VEGETABLES

Ingredients

2 lemons, sliced
2 potatoes
3 carrots
2 Roma tomatoes, sliced
1 C. sliced mushrooms
1 green, red or yellow bell
    pepper, seeded and sliced
1 onion, chopped
½ lb. fresh green beans
Olive oil
2 tsp. minced garlic
Salt and pepper to taste
Cayenne pepper, optional

Directions

Cut two (20") pieces of heavy-duty aluminum foil and stack them together; fold up edges to hold ingredients. Arrange lemon slices down center of foil. Cut potatoes and carrots into small cubes and place over lemon slices. Stack tomatoes, mushrooms, bell pepper, onion and green beans on top. Drizzle with oil; sprinkle with garlic, salt, pepper and cayenne pepper, if desired. Add ¼ cup water or two ice cubes.

Wrap foil around vegetables, sealing well. Set on hot coals and cook for 30 minutes or until vegetables are tender. Rotate pack and turn as needed for even heat.

ONION CAROUSEL

Makes 1 serving
    1 large Vidalia, Walla-Walla or
        Mayan Sweet onion
    Garlic powder
    Pepper
    1 slice bacon
    1 T. butter or margarine

Build a campfire. Peel the outer skin from each onion and cut an "X" from the top of the onion to within 1" from the bottom. Cut another "X" from the top of the onion to make 8 sections, keeping sections attached at the bottom. Sprinkle onion with garlic powder and pepper to taste. Cut bacon slice in half lengthwise. Weave bacon pieces in a criss-cross pattern between wedges. Place butter on top of onion and wrap onion in a double layer of aluminum foil. Place wrapped onion directly in the coals of the campfire and cook for 45 minutes, turning every 15 minutes. Using long tongs, remove onion from fire. Using a hot pad or oven mitt, slowly unwrap onion.

SPICED-APPLE SWEET POTATOES

Ingredients
    1 (15 oz.) can sweet potatoes, drained
    ¼ C. apple butter
    2 T. brown sugar
    ¼ tsp. ground cinnamon
    1 T. butter, cut into pieces

Directions
Cut one (18") square of heavy-duty aluminum foil and fold edges up slightly to hold ingredients. Place sweet potatoes on foil; set aside. In a bowl, stir together apple butter, brown sugar, cinnamon and 1 tablespoon water. Spoon mixture over sweet potatoes. Dot with pieces of butter.

Wrap foil around food, sealing well. Place pack on grate over medium coals, seam side up, and cook for 10 to 20 minutes or until heated through. Rotate pack as needed for even heat. Divvy up the 'taters among three or four people.

CHILI CHEESE FRIES

Makes 4 servings

1 (26 oz.) bag frozen French fries
1 (15 oz.) can chili with beans
1 (15 oz.) jar Cheez Whiz

Build a campfire. Place frozen French fries, chili with beans and Cheez Whiz on a large piece of aluminum foil. You may have to divide ingredients into two packets. Mix ingredients together slightly and wrap aluminum up and over fries to seal the packet. Wrap packet(s) again in aluminum foil. Place wrapped packet(s) directly in the coals of the campfire and cook for 20 to 25 minutes, until fries are softened and cooked. Using long tongs, remove packet from fire. Using a hot pad or oven mitt, slowly unwrap packet(s).

Quick Tip:

"Although it may seem excessive to double-bag everything or bring only tested leak-proof containers, imagine a spilled container of garlic salt in your main food barrel. ... There is nothing worse than 21 days of garlic salt-flavored everything." (from *Camp Cooking in the Wild* by Mark Scriver, Wendy Grater and Joanna Baker)

BASIL LOAF

Ingredients

½ C. butter, softened
¼ C. chopped fresh basil (or parsley)
1 (16" to 19") loaf French bread

Directions

In a small bowl, mix butter and basil until blended. Cover and let stand for at least 30 minutes to blend flavors.

Cut bread into 1" slices and spread with butter-basil mixture. Put slices back into a loaf shape (or divide into two smaller loaf shapes); wrap tightly with heavy-duty aluminum foil. Set wrapped loaf on embers (or on a grate over hot coals) and cook for 10 to 15 minutes or until bread is hot and butter is melted. Turn pack occasionally during cooking

BASIC POTATO PACK

Ingredients
1 onion, sliced
4 potatoes
¼ C. butter, cut into pieces
1 tsp. garlic salt
Salt and pepper to taste

Directions
Cut one (18") piece of heavy-duty aluminum foil. Arrange half of onion slices down center of foil. Wash potatoes and cut into thin slices. Arrange potatoes over onions; top with remaining onions. Scatter butter pieces over the top and sprinkle with garlic salt, salt and pepper. Wrap foil around vegetables and seal well. Wrap in another layer of foil, if desired. Place on hot coals and cook for 45 to 60 minutes or until potatoes are tender. Rotate and turn pack over several times during cooking. Open to serve four.

Get Cheesy: Use ingredients listed for Basic Potato Pack, but cut potatoes into long thin strips, like French fries. Place potatoes on a double layer of heavy-duty foil, sprinkle with seasonings and add 2 tablespoons grated Parmesan or Romano cheese. Fold up foil edges and drizzle with 1 tablespoon milk. Wrap foil around food and cook as directed. Before serving, sprinkle potatoes with more cheese.

Get Cheesier!: Use ingredients listed for Basic Potato pack plus yellow mustard and shredded American, Velveeta or Cheddar cheese. Alternate three layers of onion, potatoes, cheese, butter and a little mustard; sprinkle with seasonings, wrap in foil and cook as directed.

Make It Sweet: Wash, peel and slice two baking potatoes and two sweet potatoes. Place a few onion slices on foil and layer potatoes on top. Sprinkle with dried rosemary and salt. Add butter, wrap foil around food and cook as directed.

Quick & Easy: Drain two 16-ounce cans potatoes and toss with olive oil. Sprinkle with 2 tablespoons each dried rosemary, garlic powder and paprika. Season with salt and pepper; toss well. Wrap in foil and cook for 10 to 15 minutes or until hot.

ORANGE SLICE DELIGHTS

Ingredients
1 whole orange per person
Brown sugar
Vanilla ice cream, optional

Directions
Peel orange and cut into even slices. Cut one (12") piece of heavy-duty aluminum foil. Place two orange slices side by side in the center of foil and sprinkle with brown sugar. Set two more orange slices on top and sprinkle with more brown sugar. Repeat with remaining slices. Wrap foil around fruit, sealing well.

Set foil pack in hot coals for about 20 minutes or until oranges are hot and juicy, rotating and turning several times during cooking. Serve with ice cream, if desired.

BANANA BOATS

Makes 6 servings
6 large bananas
2 C. chocolate chips
1 (10½ oz.) pkg. miniature marshmallows

Build a campfire. Set out six large pieces of aluminum foil. Leaving the peels on the bananas, remove the stems. Make a cut in each banana from top to bottom lengthwise. Spoon out a little of the banana flesh. Stuff with chocolate chips and marshmallows. Wrap each banana in aluminum foil. Place wrapped bananas directly in the coals of the campfire and cook for about 5 minutes, until chocolate is melted. Using long tongs, remove bananas from fire. Using a hot pad or oven mitt, slowly unwrap bananas. Eat banana boats with a spoon right from the peel.

PEARS IN CARAMEL SAUCE

Makes 2 servings
2 T. sweetened butter
2 T. brown sugar
Pinch of cinnamon
1 Comice or Anjou pear
1 orange, halved

Build a campfire. Set out two large pieces of aluminum foil. Cut pear in half and remove core and stem. In a small bowl, combine butter, brown sugar and cinnamon. Lay each pear half on a piece of the aluminum foil. Scoop half of the butter mixture into the cored side of each pear. Squeeze orange juice over each pear. Wrap aluminum foil up around pears and seal tightly. Place wrapped pears directly in the coals of the campfire and cook for about 20 to 30 minutes, until completely softened. Using long tongs, remove packets from fire. Using a hot pad or oven mitt, slowly unwrap packets, being careful not to spill hot caramel sauce.

Quick Tip:
For foods you wish to cook with plenty of steam, make a tent-like pack, leaving some room between the top of the food and the foil. A tent pack is good for vegetables, fruits and combination packs that need less browning.

PIE IRON

A pie iron is made of two cast-iron or aluminum pans connected by a hinge and two long sticks. It is just the perfect size for making a sandwich or using bread to make some other tasty treat over the fire. It can also be used like a miniature skillet. Pie irons and the tasty foods made in them are known throughout the world, and are called by many names, including: sandwich cooker/toaster, mountain pie, pudgy pie iron, jaffle iron, panini grill, toasties, and even hobo pie.

Cast-iron pie irons need to be "seasoned" before use. Typically, this means rubbing a small amount of vegetable shortening on the inside and outside of the iron, then setting the cooking end in the fire for up to an hour. After the iron cools, wash with plain water and lightly grease again before storing. (Check manufacturer's directions for seasoning your particular iron).

Quick Tip:
Remember to turn pie irons often when cooking to reduce the chance of charred food.

TOASTY BACON & EGG SANDWICH

Ingredients
1 egg
2 slices bread
1 strip bacon
1 slice cheese
Butter

Directions
In a small bowl, beat egg slightly. Butter one side of each slice of bread.

Spray pie iron with nonstick cooking spray. Cut bacon strip crosswise in four pieces and lay pieces on one side of iron, covering as much of the iron as possible. Cover bacon with a slice of bread, buttered side down. Carefully pour beaten egg on bread and add cheese. Add remaining bread slice, buttered side up.

Close iron and trim off any excess bread around the outside. Hold iron over hot coals for 4 to 6 minutes or until bread is toasted, turning often.

HASH BROWN PIE

Makes 1 serving
1 C. frozen hash browns, thawed
½ C. chopped onions
1 tsp. garlic salt
Pepper to taste

Build a flaming campfire. Generously grease both sides of the pie iron with non-stick cooking spray. In a medium bowl, combine thawed hash browns, chopped onions and garlic salt. Mix well and season with pepper to taste. Pat hash browns mixture into a square and set on one side of the pie iron. Close iron and hold over flames for 8 to 10 minutes. Remove iron from fire and open carefully with a hot pad or oven mitt.

FIRED-UP FRITTATA

Ingredients

1 egg
Milk
1 strip bacon
Frozen hash browns, thawed
Purchased broccoli slaw
Shredded Cheddar cheese
Salt, pepper and Italian seasoning to taste
Chopped tomato, optional
Sour cream, optional

Directions

Spray pie iron with nonstick cooking spray. In a small bowl, beat egg with 1 tablespoon milk. Cut bacon strip crosswise into four pieces and lay pieces on one side of iron, covering as much of the iron as possible. Cover bacon with a single layer of hash browns. Add 1 tablespoon broccoli slaw. Carefully pour beaten egg on top, keeping it away from edge of iron. Spray egg with nonstick cooking spray.

Close iron and hold over hot coals without turning for 7 to 8 minutes or until egg is cooked. Remove from iron and immediately sprinkle with cheese and seasonings. Garnish with tomato and sour cream for a little extra pizzazz!

FRENCH TOASTIES

Ingredients

1 egg
¼ C. milk
2 slices bread
Maple syrup to taste

Directions

Thoroughly spray pie iron with nonstick cooking spray. In a small bowl, whisk together egg and milk until thoroughly mixed. Dip one side of one bread slice in egg mixture and place it egg side down in pie iron. Drizzle with maple syrup. Dip one side of the second bread slice in egg mixture and place it egg side up in iron.

Close iron and trim off any excess bread around the outside. Hold iron over embers for 4 to 6 minutes or until bread is toasted, turning often. Makes one yummy breakfast.

CINNAMON OR GARLIC BISCUITS

Makes 8 servings
1 tube of 8 buttermilk biscuits
2 T. butter, melted
Cinnamon and sugar mixture
   OR 2 tsp. garlic salt

Build a flaming campfire. Generously grease both sides of the pie iron with non-stick cooking spray. Separate tube into individual biscuits. Roll each biscuit into a ball. Place either cinnamon and sugar mixture or garlic salt in a shallow bowl. Brush biscuits with melted butter and then roll in either cinnamon and sugar mixture or garlic salt. Place one biscuit ball on pie iron. Close iron and hold over flames for about 5 minutes, or until biscuit is golden brown. Remove iron from fire and open carefully with a hot pad or oven mitt. Repeat with remaining ingredients.

Quick Tip:
Prepare cinnamon and sugar mixture at home by combining 2 tablespoons sugar and 1 teaspoon cinnamon. Pack in an airtight container until ready to prepare recipe.

PUDGIE POP-TARTS

Ingredients
2 slices bread
Butter
Fruit preserves, any kind
Canned vanilla frosting

Directions
Butter one side of each bread slice. Place one slice buttered side down in a hot pie iron. Top with about 2 tablespoons preserves and another bread slice, buttered side up.

Close iron and trim off excess bread around the outside. Cook about 4 minutes or until bread is toasted, turning occasionally. Remove from iron and spread with about 1 tablespoon frosting for one serving.

Use more bread, preserves and frosting to make a bunch of these!

BREAKFAST EGG & SAUSAGE MUFFINS

Makes 8 servings

8 English muffins, split in half
1 lb. sausage patties
8 to 10 eggs, scrambled and cooked
½ C. shredded cheese, any kind
Salt and pepper to taste

Build a flaming campfire. Generously grease both sides of the pie iron with non-stick cooking spray. Place one English muffin half on each side of a pie iron. Place 1 sausage patty, a little of the precooked scrambled eggs and 1 tablespoon shredded cheese on one English muffin half. Sprinkle with salt and pepper to taste. Top with another English muffin half and close pie iron. Hold pie iron over the fire, turning occasionally, for 5 to 7 minutes. Remove iron from fire and open carefully with a hot pad or oven mitt. Repeat with remaining ingredients.

Quick Tip:
Prepare scrambled eggs at home by whisking together 8 to 10 eggs and 2 tablespoons milk. Cook eggs over medium heat and pack in an airtight container. Place in cooler until ready to prepare recipe.

BELGIAN PIE

Ingredients

1 (4 ct.) tube refrigerated crescent rolls
2. T. cream cheese, softened, divided
2. T. applesauce, divided

Directions

Spray two pie irons with nonstick cooking spray. Press together seams of two crescent roll triangles, flattening to make a 5" x 8" rectangle. Cut in half to make two 5" x 4" pieces. Place one piece on one side of iron. Spread 1 tablespoon cream cheese and 1 tablespoon applesauce on dough. Top with another piece of dough. Repeat with remaining ingredients in the other pie iron.

Close irons and trim off any excess dough around the outside. Cook over hot coals for 3 to 4 minutes or until dough is toasty brown. Serves two.

HASH & EGGS

Ingredients
1 hard-cooked egg
2 slices bread
Butter
Canned hash

Directions
Chop hard-cooked egg. Butter one side of each bread slice and place one in a pie iron, buttered side down. Top with egg and 1 to 2 tablespoons hash. Top with the other bread slice, buttered side up.

Close iron and trim off any excess bread around the outside. Cook over hot coals for 4 minutes or until hot, turning occasionally. Use the rest of the hash plus more bread and eggs to make additional servings.

FRIED EGGS

Ingredients
2 eggs
Salt and pepper to taste

Directions
You'll need a pie iron that comes apart completely at the hinges for this recipe. Unhinge iron and spray heavily with nonstick cooking spray. Place empty iron halves over the fire to get them hot. Place an egg on each half; add salt and pepper. Hold each section upright over embers until eggs are cooked to desired doneness, breaking yolks if needed.

Variation
For scrambled eggs, keep pie iron hinged, beat 1 egg with a little milk and pour carefully into hot iron. Close iron without turning and hold over embers until egg is cooked.

LITTLE WAFFLE CASSEROLE

Ingredients

Butter
Frozen waffles
Egg whites
American cheese slices
Sausage, ham, or bacon,
    cooked and chopped

Directions

Put a frozen waffle into a buttered pie iron. Slowly pour an egg white over the waffle, letting it seep into the crevices. Top with a slice of American cheese and cover the cheese with a layer of cooked and chopped sausage, ham and/or bacon. Close the iron and hold it over hot embers without flipping, until the egg is cooked and the cheese is melted. Make as many as you need.

APPLESAUCE PANCAKES

Ingredients

1 C. biscuit baking mix
½ tsp. cinnamon
1 egg
½ C. applesauce
½ tsp. lemon juice
¼ C. milk

Directions

Combine baking mix, cinnamon, egg, applesauce, lemon juice and milk. Stir until the lumps are nearly gone.

Fill one side of a greased pie iron with batter. Hold level while cooking in warm coals; don't flip iron until the batter has thickened up nicely. Cook until both sides are brown.

Serve with syrup and applesauce.

POTATO-BACON PANCAKES

Ingredients

2 C. frozen shredded hash browns, thawed
1 egg
Green onions, chopped
Bacon, cooked and crumbled
Shredded Cheddar cheese
Garlic salt
Black pepper
Sour cream

Directions

Grease a pie iron. Mix potatoes and egg. Add some chopped green onions and bacon; stir in some cheese. Pack potato mixture tightly into one side of your iron. Sprinkle with garlic salt and pepper.

Close the pie iron and set in warm coals until toasted on one side; flip until brown on the other side and heated all the way through. Top with sour cream and more green onions and cheese, as desired.

REUBEN PIE

Ingredients
Butter
2 slices rye bread
2 thin slices corned beef
Sauerkraut, drained
1 slice Swiss cheese

Directions
Butter one side of each bread slice; put one slice buttered side down on pie iron. Layer corned beef, 1 tablespoon sauerkraut and Swiss cheese on bread. Put the other bread slice on top, buttered side up.

Close iron and trim off any excess bread around the outside. Hold iron over hot coals for 4 to 6 minutes or until bread is toasted, turning often. This Reuben will make one lucky camper very happy!

TACO TENTS

Makes 4 servings
2 tubes of 8 refrigerated crescent rolls
1 lb. prepared taco meat
2 C. shredded cheese, any kind
Salsa, tomatoes, lettuce and/
    or sour cream, optional

Build a flaming campfire. Generously grease both sides of the pie iron with non-stick cooking spray. Unroll crescent rolls and separate into squares, leaving every two crescent rolls together. There should be 8 squares. Place one square on one side of the pie iron. Spoon some of the prepared taco meat and shredded cheese onto square. Top with another crescent roll square. Close iron and hold over flames for 3 minutes on each side, until crescent squares are golden brown. Remove iron from fire and open carefully with a hot pad or oven mitt. If desired, garnish tacos with salsa, tomatoes, lettuce and/or sour cream. Repeat with remaining ingredients.

Quick Tip:
Prepare taco meat at home by browning 1 pound ground beef and mixing with ½ cup water and 1 envelope of taco seasoning. Pack in an airtight container and place in cooler until ready to prepare recipe.

POT PIE

Ingredients

Butter
2 slices bread
Canned beef or chicken stew

Directions

Butter one side of each bread slice. Place one slice buttered side down in pie iron. Place about 2 tablespoons stew on bread. Top with second slice of bread, buttered side up.

Close iron and trim off any excess bread around the outside. Hold iron over hot coals for 4 to 6 minutes or until bread is toasted, turning often.

BBQ CHICKEN PIE

Ingredients

Italian bread, sliced
Butter
Thinly-sliced deli chicken breast
Canadian bacon, sliced
Monterrey Jack cheese, sliced
BBQ Sauce to taste

Directions

For each pie, butter two slices of bread on one side only; place one slice buttered side down in pie iron. Layer 1 slice each of chicken breast, Canadian bacon and Monterrey Jack cheese on top. Drizzle with BBQ sauce. Add the second slice of bread, buttered side up.

Close iron and trim off any excess bread around the outside. Hold iron over hot coals about 4 to 6 minutes or until bread is toasted, turning often.

MEAT & CHEESE MELTS

Makes 2 servings

2 slices American or Swiss cheese
4 slices white or wheat bread
4 slices deli style ham, turkey or roast beef

Build a flaming campfire. Generously grease both sides of the pie iron with non-stick cooking spray. Assemble sandwich by placing one cheese slice on one slice of bread. Top with 2 slices of ham, turkey or roast beef and another slice of bread. Place sandwich on one side of the pie iron. Close iron and hold over flames for 3 minutes on each side. Remove iron from fire and open carefully with a hot pad or oven mitt. Repeat with remaining ingredients.

MEXICAN PIE

Ingredients
6" flour tortillas
Refried beans
Shredded Cheddar cheese
Taco seasoning or chili powder to taste
Salsa

Directions
Spray pie iron with nonstick cooking spray. Place a flour tortilla on one side of iron. Spread 2 to 3 tablespoons refried beans in the middle of the tortilla. Sprinkle with 1 tablespoon Cheddar cheese and taco seasoning or chili powder. Place another tortilla over the top.

Close iron and trim off any excess tortilla around the outside. Hold iron over hot coals for about 4 to 6 minutes or until heated through, turning often. Serve with salsa.

GRILLED ROAST BEEF

Makes 5 servings
1 (4 oz.) can chopped green chiles, drained
2 T. mayonnaise
1 T. Dijon mustard
10 slices rye bread
5 slices Swiss cheese
10 slices deli style roast beef
Salsa or Picante sauce, optional

Build a flaming campfire. Generously grease both sides of the pie iron with non-stick cooking spray. In a small bowl, combine chopped green chiles, mayonnaise and Dijon mustard. Spread mixture on one side of each slice of bread. Assemble sandwich by placing one Swiss cheese slice on the spread side of one slice of bread. Top with 2 slices of beef and another slice of bread, spread side down. Place sandwich on one side of the pie iron. Close iron and hold over flames for 3 minutes on each side. Remove iron from fire and open carefully with a hot pad or oven mitt. If desired, serve with salsa or Picante sauce. Repeat with remaining ingredients.

Quick Tip:
Prepare spread at home by combining chopped green chiles, mayonnaise and Dijon mustard. Pack in an airtight container and place in cooler until ready to prepare recipe.

CAMP RAVIOLI & GARLIC TOAST

Ingredients

Butter
1 (8 ct.) pkg. frozen garlic-flavored
Texas toast, thawed*
1 (15 oz.) can ravioli

Directions

Butter one side of each toast slice. Place one slice buttered side down in pie iron. Place about three ravioli pieces and a little sauce on top of toast. Top with remaining toast slice, buttered side up.

Close iron and trim off any excess bread around the outside. Hold iron over hot coals for 4 to 6 minutes or until bread is toasted, turning often. Serves four.

Variation

Use about ¼ cup canned or homemade spaghetti and sauce in place of ravioli.

* You may need to slice each piece if it's too thick.

PIZZA POCKETS

Makes 2 servings

1 T. butter, softened
4 slices white bread
¼ C. pizza sauce
12 to 18 pepperoni slices
1 (4 oz.) can sliced mushrooms, drained
½ C. shredded mozzarella cheese

Build a flaming campfire. Generously grease both sides of the pie iron with non-stick cooking spray. Spread butter over one side of each slice of bread. Place one slice of bread, buttered side out, into one side of the pie iron. Layer half of the pizza sauce, pepperoni slices, mushrooms and shredded mozzarella cheese onto bread slice. Cover with another slice of bread, buttered side out. Close iron and hold over flames for 3 minutes on each side. Remove iron from fire and open carefully with a hot pad or oven mitt. Repeat with remaining ingredients.

HOT HAM & SWISS ON RYE

Ingredients
- 2 slices rye bread
- 2 thin slices deli ham
- 1 slice Swiss cheese
- Yellow mustard to taste

Directions
Butter one side of each bread slice and place one slice in pie iron buttered side down. Top with ham and cheese slice. Spread a little mustard over cheese and top with the other bread slice, buttered side up.

Close iron and trim off any excess bread around the outside. Hold iron over hot coals about 4 to 6 minutes or until bread is toasted, turning often.

Variation
Change it up by using your favorite bread, deli meat, cheese and condiments.

SALMON PATTIES

Ingredients
- 1 (14.7 oz.) can salmon
- 1 green onion
- 1 (1 oz.) pkg. Ranch dressing mix
- 1 (10.7 oz.) can cream of mushroom soup

Directions
Spray both sides of a pie iron with nonstick cooking spray. Drain and remove bones from salmon. Thinly slice green onion. In a small bowl, stir together salmon, onion, dressing mix and soup. Divide mixture evenly into six portions and place one portion in iron. Add 1 teaspoon water.

Close iron and cook over hot coals until patties are brown and crunchy on the outside, turning often.

TUNA MELTS

Ingredients

1 tomato
1 (7 oz.) can tuna, drained
⅓ C. mayonnaise
1 T. Parmesan cheese
3 T. sweet pickle relish
2 tsp. dried parsley
1 tsp. dried dill weed
Garlic powder to taste
Onion powder to taste
Butter
12 slices bread
6 slices Havarti cheese

Directions

Spray pie iron with nonstick cooking spray. Cut tomato into six slices. In a small bowl, stir together tuna, mayonnaise, Parmesan cheese, pickle relish, parsley, dill weed and garlic and onion powders. Divide mixture into six equal portions. Spread butter on one side of each bread slice. Place one bread slice buttered side down in iron. Spread one portion of tuna mixture onto bread. Add a slice of Havarti cheese and tomato. Top with another bread slice, buttered side up.

Close iron and trim off any excess bread around the outside. Hold iron over hot coals about 4 to 6 minutes or until bread is toasted, turning often.

HILLBILLY BURRITO

Makes 4 servings

1 lb. prepared taco meat
½ C. salsa
2 C. shredded Cheddar cheese
4 burrito size tortillas

Build a flaming campfire. Generously grease both sides of the pie iron with non-stick cooking spray. Place 1 tortilla on the pie iron. The tortilla should be large enough to cover both sides of the open pie iron. Spoon some of the prepared taco meat, salsa and shredded cheese onto one side of the tortilla. Fold remaining half of the tortilla over the filling and fold edges in to make a square packet. Close iron and hold over flames for 3 minutes on each side, until tortilla is golden brown. Remove iron from fire and open carefully with a hot pad or oven mitt. Repeat with remaining ingredients.

Quick Tip:

Prepare taco meat at home by browning 1 pound ground beef and mixing with ½ cup water and 1 envelope of taco seasoning. Pack in an airtight container and place in cooler until ready to prepare recipe.

SECOND-HAND 'WICHES

Ingredients
Any leftover grilled meat
Any vegetables, like onion or
    bell pepper, seeded
Butter
2 bread slices
Any cheese, sliced, shredded or grated
Italian dressing to taste
Garlic powder to taste
Dried oregano to taste

Directions
Thinly slice meat and vegetables. Butter one side of each slice of bread. Put one slice buttered side down in a pie iron. Layer on meat, vegetables and cheese. Drizzle with a little dressing and sprinkle with garlic powder and oregano. Place the other bread slice on top, buttered side up.

Close iron and trim off any excess bread around the outside. Hold iron over hot coals for 4 to 6 minutes or until bread is toasted, turning often.

Keep making sandwiches until all the leftovers are gone.

GRILLED CHEESE PERFECTION

Makes 1 serving
1 T. butter, softened
2 slices white bread
2 slices American or Cheddar cheese
1 slice tomato

Build a flaming campfire. Generously grease both sides of the pie iron with non-stick cooking spray. Spread butter over one side of each slice of bread. Place one slice of bread, buttered side out, into one side of the pie iron. Layer with one cheese slice, tomato slice and remaining cheese slice. Cover with remaining slice of bread, buttered side out. Close iron and hold over flames for 3 minutes on each side. Remove iron from fire and open carefully with a hot pad or oven mitt.

EASY TOTS

Ingredients
Onion
Frozen tater tots, thawed
Garlic salt, pepper and salt to taste
Shredded Cheddar cheese

Directions
Spray pie iron with nonstick cooking spray. Finely chop onion. Arrange a layer of tater tots on one side of iron. Add 1 teaspoon onion. Season with garlic salt, pepper and salt.

Close iron and hold over embers for 4 to 5 minutes on each side. Open iron by keeping parallel to the ground and lifting one side. Sprinkle with cheese. Close and cook, cheese side up, 1 minute more, without turning.

VEGGIE MEDLEY

Ingredients
Zucchini
Green or red bell pepper
Tomato
Italian dressing

Directions
Spray pie iron with nonstick cooking spray. Thinly slice zucchini, bell pepper and tomato. Layer vegetables to fill one side of iron. Drizzle with 1 tablespoon dressing.

Close iron and hold over embers for 3 to 4 minutes on each side until veggies are cooked.

Make lots of these to use up your veggies. And besides, they're good for you!

PORTABELLA MELT

Ingredients
Butter
1 large portabella mushroom cap
1 slice mozzarella cheese

Directions
Generously grease both sides of pie iron with butter. Place the mushroom in iron.

Close iron and hold over embers for 2 to 3 minutes on each side. Open iron so bottom side of mushroom is face up. Tuck cheese inside mushroom, close iron and cook 1 to 2 minutes more, without turning.

CORNBREAD PIZZAZZ

Ingredients
1 (7 oz.) pkg. corn muffin mix
Egg and milk as directed on muffin package
1 (4 oz.) can chile peppers, drained
½ C. shredded Cheddar cheese
¼ C. chopped onion

Directions
In a small bowl, stir together corn muffin mix, egg and milk as directed on package. Stir in chile peppers, cheese and onion.

Heavily spray pie iron with nonstick cooking spray. Fill one side of iron about ⅓ full with batter. Close iron and cook over embers for several minutes until cooked through, turning often.

STUFFED CORNBREAD

Ingredients

1 (8.5 oz.) pkg. corn muffin mix, pre-mixed
   and baked in a greased 9" x 13" pan
Prepared chili
Shredded Pepper Jack cheese
Sour cream, optional

Directions

Grease your pie iron and cut cornbread to fit. For each, layer one cornbread piece, some chili, a little cheese and another cornbread piece. If your cornbread pieces crumble, just push them together to fit in your pie iron. Close iron and cook, checking occasionally, until nicely toasted on both sides. Serve with sour cream.

ONION PUFFS

Ingredients

Puff pastry
Onion slices
Swiss cheese
Cheddar cheese
Salt and pepper

Directions

Generously grease a pie iron. Cut pastry a bit smaller than the iron; stretch to fit inside. Add an onion slice, cheeses, salt, and pepper. Place second pastry piece on top; seal edges.

   Close iron and cook over warm coals, turning often (if dough oozes out, just trim it off). When it looks like a little golden pillow, it's done.

LEMON CHIFFON PIE

Ingredients
Butter
Bread
Lemon pie filling
Marshmallows

Directions
Butter one side of each slice of bread; put one slice buttered side down on the pie iron. Put about ¼ cup pie filling on bread and top with several marshmallows. Put the other slice of bread on top, buttered side up.

Close iron and trim off any excess bread around the outside. Hold iron over embers for 4 to 6 minutes or until bread is toasted, turning often.

PINEAPPLE UPSIDE-DOWN CAKE

Ingredients
4 cake donuts
Butter
4 pineapple slices
Brown sugar to taste

Directions
Slice donut in half horizontally. Butter the cut sides. Put one donut half buttered side down on a pie iron. Top with a pineapple slice and sprinkle with brown sugar. Put another donut half on top, buttered side up.

Close iron and hold over embers for 4 to 6 minutes or until donut is golden brown. Repeat with remaining donuts and pineapple slices. Whether or not you share them is up to you.

APPLE OR CHERRY TURNOVERS

Makes 4 servings

2 T. butter, softened
8 slices white bread
1 (12 oz.) can apple or cherry pie filling

Build a flaming campfire. Generously grease both sides of the pie iron with non-stick cooking spray. Spread butter over one side of each slice of bread. Place one slice of bread, buttered side out, into one side of the pie iron. Spoon some of the apple or cherry pie filling into the center of the bread slice. Cover with another slice of bread, buttered side out. Close iron and hold over flames for 2 to 3 minutes on each side. Remove iron from fire and open carefully with a hot pad or oven mitt. Repeat with remaining ingredients.

PEANUT BUTTER CHOCOLATE TREATS

Makes 2 servings

1 T. butter, softened
4 slices white bread
3 T. creamy or crunchy peanut butter
¼ C. chocolate chips

Build a flaming campfire. Generously grease both sides of the pie iron with non-stick cooking spray. Spread butter over one side of each slice of bread. Place one slice of bread, buttered side out, into one side of the pie iron. Spread half of the peanut butter over the bread slice. Sprinkle half of the chocolate chips over the peanut butter. Cover with another slice of bread, buttered side out. Close iron and hold over flames for 2 to 3 minutes on each side. Remove iron from fire and open carefully with a hot pad or oven mitt. Repeat with remaining ingredients.

SWEET PEACH POCKET

Makes 1 serving

2 slices white bread
1 T. butter, softened
1 peach half, pitted
1 marshmallow
Powdered sugar

Build a flaming campfire. Generously grease both sides of the pie iron with non-stick cooking spray. Spread butter over one side of each slice of bread. Place one slice of bread, buttered side out, into one side of the pie iron. Lay peach half over bread slice and place marshmallow inside the pitted peach. Top with remaining slice of bread, buttered side out. Close iron and hold over flames for 2 to 3 minutes on each side. Remove iron from fire and open carefully with a hot pad or oven mitt. Dust with powdered sugar.

Try this

Try using refrigerated pie crust in place of bread. Cut crust to fit in pie iron and butter as you would bread slices. Cook as directed until crust is lightly browned.

BANANA RAFTS

Makes 2 servings

1 T. butter, softened
4 slices white bread
3 T. creamy or crunchy peanut butter
1 banana, peeled
1 to 2 T. brown sugar

Build a flaming campfire. Generously grease both sides of the pie iron with non-stick cooking spray. Spread butter over one side of each slice of bread. Place one slice of bread, buttered side out, into one side of the pie iron. Spread half of the peanut butter over the bread slice. Slice banana in half lengthwise and then cut each side in half. There should be 4 banana pieces. Lay 2 of the banana pieces over peanut butter and sprinkle with half of the brown sugar. Cover with another slice of bread, buttered side out. Close iron and hold over flames for 2 to 3 minutes on each side. Remove iron from fire and open carefully with a hot pad or oven mitt. Repeat with remaining ingredients.

DREAM PIES

Ingredients
Refrigerated flaky biscuits
Butter, melted
Cinnamon sugar
Raspberry jam
Lemon pie filling

Directions
Flatten a biscuit and coat with butter and sprinkle with cinnamon sugar. Fit into pie iron; spread with jam and pie filling.

Top with another coated biscuit; press edges together. Close iron and cook in warm coals until biscuits are done.

Garnish any way you'd like or enjoy plain.

CARAMEL APPLE ANGEL PIES

Ingredients
Angel food cake
Apples
Caramel dip
Chopped peanuts
Cinnamon sugar

Directions
Set one cake slice in a generously greased pie iron. Cover with thinly sliced apples, caramel dip, peanuts and a generous dose of cinnamon sugar.

Add another cake slice. Close the iron; cook slowly in warm coals until the cake has browned evenly.

SKILLET

Cooking in a skillet is one of the easier ways to make a meal over a fire. Simply nestle the skillet into hot coals or set it up on empty cans or a grate. Your food is contained within the skillet, so it's hard to lose morsels into the flames! Skillets are great for meals using ground meat and other foods that you want to brown. They're also a good way to keep food warm for a bit—just cover the skillet with foil.

Quick Tip:

Pack raw eggs in a cooler with lots of ice. Put the cooler in the shade and don't open it unnecessarily. The food will stay refrigerator-cold as long as the ice lasts. If hiking, buy dried eggs from the supermarket or sporting goods store and reconstitute them with purified water.

APPLE-RAISIN PANCAKES

Ingredients

1 (7 oz.) pkg. apple-cinnamon muffin mix
1 egg
1 T. vegetable oil
¼ C. raisins
Maple syrup or powdered sugar

Directions

Grease a skillet with nonstick cooking spray and set aside. In a medium bowl, combine muffin mix, egg and ⅓ cup water; beat until smooth. Stir in oil and raisins. Place skillet over embers until heated; spoon batter on hot skillet and cook pancakes until bubbly around edges; flip over gently and cook until lightly browned and cooked through. Serve with syrup or powdered sugar.

CORN FRITTERS

Ingredients

2 eggs, beaten
½ C. milk
2 tsp. dried minced onion
1 tsp. celery seed
¼ tsp. pepper
¼ tsp. salt, optional
1¼ C. biscuit baking mix
1 (15 oz.) can whole kernel corn, drained
Vegetable oil for frying
Maple syrup or honey

Directions

In a medium bowl, whisk together eggs, milk, onion, celery seed, pepper and salt, if desired. Stir in baking mix and corn until blended. Place a skillet over hot coals. Heat 3 tablespoons oil until a drop of batter sizzles. Drop batter by the spoonful into hot oil. Brown fritters on one side, 6 to 8 minutes, flip and brown the other side; add additional oil as needed. Serve warm with syrup or honey to satisfy four to six hungry campers.

SWEET CEREAL SLICES

Ingredients

4 C. Special K cereal
1 C. sugar
1 C. light corn syrup
1 (12 oz.) jar creamy peanut butter

Directions

Place cereal in a large bowl. Set skillet on hot coals and add sugar and syrup. Bring mixture to a boil; stir in peanut butter. Carefully remove skillet from heat; pour mixture over cereal in bowl. Stir well to coat cereal. With hands, roll mixture into 12" logs. Cut into 1" slices.

BREAKFAST BISCUITS

Ingredients
1 C. flour
2 tsp. baking powder
½ tsp. salt
1½ T. sugar
1 T. butter or shortening (not margarine)
3 T. real bacon bits
1 tsp. maple flavoring, optional
Butter

Directions
Before leaving home, stir together flour, baking powder, salt and sugar; store in a zippered plastic bag or airtight storage container. Wrap the butter and bacon bits separately in plastic wrap and add to bag with dry ingredients.

To prepare biscuits, pour dry ingredients into a bowl. Mix butter into flour mixture with fingertips until crumbly. Add bacon bits. Stir in ½ cup water and maple flavoring, if desired, until a soft dough forms. Do not knead. Shape dough into biscuits and place in a skillet. Set skillet on a grate over hot coals. Cook biscuits until golden brown on the bottom; flip biscuits over and cook until browned and no longer doughy. Serve with butter.

FLAPJACKS

Ingredients
2 C. flour
1 tsp. baking powder
½ tsp. baking soda
1 tsp. salt
2 tsp. sugar
¼ C. butter, melted
2 eggs
2 C. buttermilk
Fruit, nuts, chocolate chips, optional
Maple syrup

Directions
Before leaving home, stir together flour, baking powder, baking soda, salt and sugar; store in a zippered plastic bag or airtight storage container.

In a medium bowl, whisk together butter, eggs and buttermilk. Add dry pancake mix from plastic bag; whisk until almost smooth. Grease skillet with nonstick cooking spray and set over medium-hot coals until a drop of water sizzles. Pour batter onto skillet to make small pancakes; sprinkle with fruit, nuts or chocolate chips, if desired. When edges are bubbly, flip pancakes gently and cook until lightly browned and cooked through. Serve with syrup.

ORANGE-BLUEBERRY OATMEAL

Ingredients
¾ C. old-fashioned oats
¼ C. dried blueberries
¼ C. chopped pecans
1¼ tsp. orange gelatin powder
2 T. nonfat dry milk
⅛ tsp. salt

Directions
Before leaving home, stir together oats, blueberries, pecans, gelatin powder, dry milk and salt; store in a zippered plastic bag or airtight storage container for a single serving of oatmeal.

To prepare oatmeal, set a skillet over hot coals. Add 1 cup water and bring to a boil. Stir in prepared oatmeal mixture and return to a boil. Cover with foil and remove from heat; let stand 8 minutes or until water is absorbed.

Other flavor combinations
Swap out the blueberries, pecans and orange gelatin for…
- Dried cherries, walnuts and cherry gelatin
- Dried cranberries, sliced almonds and orange gelatin
- Blueberries, sliced almonds and lemon gelatin

BREAKFAST BURRITOS

Ingredients
1 T. olive oil
1 red or green bell pepper, seeded, chopped
2 C. cubed leftover potatoes
1 C. sliced fresh mushrooms
4 to 6 eggs, beaten
4 (10") flour tortillas, warmed*
1 C. shredded Cheddar cheese
Salsa and sour cream, optional

Directions
Place a skillet over hot coals to heat the oil. Add bell pepper; cook and stir for 2 minutes. Add mushrooms and cook until tender. Sprinkle in potatoes and cook until they begin to crisp, adding more oil if necessary. Add eggs and scramble them into vegetables until eggs are set. Remove skillet from heat and spoon a portion of the mixture onto each tortilla; top with cheese, salsa and sour cream as desired. Roll up to serve four.

* Wrap tortillas in foil and set over warm coals for a few minutes until warmed.

EGG CRACKLE

Makes 6 servings

1 lb. bacon, chopped
12 eggs
¼ C. milk
Salt and pepper to taste
1 individual size bag cheese crackers

Place grilling grate over campfire. Place chopped bacon in a cast iron skillet and place skillet over heat. Cook bacon to desired crispness and drain grease from skillet. In a medium bowl, combine eggs and milk. Add salt and pepper to taste. Add egg mixture to skillet and mix with bacon pieces. Cook until eggs are set. Crush cheese crackers into small pieces and sprinkle over eggs.

EARLY BIRD NESTS

Makes 2 servings

1 T. vegetable oil
2 slices white or wheat bread
2 eggs
Bacon bits
Salt and pepper to taste

Place grilling grate over campfire. Place vegetable oil in a cast iron skillet and place skillet over heat. Tear out the center of each slice of bread and set in skillet. Toast bread centers until lightly browned, turning once. Remove from skillet and set aside. Set bread crusts (with a hole in the center) in skillet and toast until lightly browned on one side. Turn crusts over and crack one egg in the center of each hole. Cook until eggs are set. Top with bacon bits. Season with salt and pepper to taste. Serve with toasted bread centers on the side.

Cooking Gear for Your Campsite

Here's a list of basic essentials you'll want to bring along for a short summer camping trip:

- Pots and pans
- Coffee pot
- Cutting board
- Cooking utensils
- Cups, bowls, plates, and cutlery

- Lighter or matches
- Firebox and thick leather work gloves, or stove and fuel in fuel bottles
- 15" folding saw
- Water filter or water treatment

- Large 1 to 1.5 gallon (4 to 6 liter) jug for treated water
- Biodegradable hand soap and dish soap
- Food!

(from *Canoe Camping* by Mark Scriver)

ICED CINNAMON SWIRL PANCAKES

Makes 6 to 8 servings

½ C. butter, melted
¾ C. brown sugar
1 T. cinnamon
2 eggs
1 C. milk
3 T. vegetable oil
1½ C. flour
¾ tsp. salt
2 tsp. baking powder
¼ C. malted milk powder or 2 T. sugar
Purchased cream cheese frosting

To make the cinnamon swirl, stir together the butter, brown sugar and cinnamon; let cool. When thickened, stir again and transfer to a zippered plastic bag; set aside.

Beat the eggs and milk together until foamy and then stir in the oil. Add the flour, salt, baking powder and malted milk powder, whisking until just combined; set aside for 15 minutes to thicken up a bit.

When you're ready to cook, grease a griddle or skillet and heat over a warm cooking fire. Use a ½-cup measuring cup to pour batter into the hot oil and to spread the batter out slightly so the pancakes aren't too thick. Immediately snip a very small corner off the bag containing the cinnamon swirl and squeeze in a spiral pattern over the pancakes; when the pancakes bubble on top and are golden brown on the bottom, flip them over and cook the other side until golden brown.

To serve, warm the frosting slightly and drizzle over the pancakes. You'll probably have some cinnamon swirl mixture left over; if so, just keep it chilled until needed again, putting a twist tie around the snipped corner.

This pancake recipe is scrumptious, but if you'd rather not make from-scratch pancakes, use the cinnamon swirl and frosting to dress up a box mix.

Campfire Singing

On Top of Old Smoky

On top of old Smoky, all covered with snow,

I lost my true lover from courting too slow.

Now, courting is pleasure and parting
is grief,

And a false-hearted lover is worse than
a thief.

For a thief will just rob you and take what
you have,

But a false-hearted lover will lead you to
the grave.

And the grave will decay you and turn you
to dust;

Not one boy in a hundred a poor girl
can trust.

They'll hug you and kiss you and tell you
more lies,

Than cross ties on a railroad or stars in
the skies.

So, come all you young maidens and listen
to me,

Never place your affection on a green
willow tree.

For the leaves they will whither, and the
roots they will die,

You'll all be forsaken and never know why.

Oh! Susanna

I come from Alabama with my banjo on
my knee,

I'm going to Louisiana, my true love for
to see.

It rained all night the day I left, the weather
it was dry.

The sun so hot I froze to death, Susanna,
don't you cry.

Chorus

Oh! Susanna, Oh don't you cry for me,

For I come from Alabama with my banjo on
my knee.

I had a dream the other night, when
everything was still;

I thought I saw Susanna dear, a coming
down the hill.

A buckwheat cake was in her mouth, a tear
was in her eye,

Says I, I'm coming from the south, Susanna,
don't you cry.

I soon will be in New Orleans, and then I'll
look around,

And when I find Susanna, I'll fall upon the
ground.

But if I do not find her, then I will surely die,

And when I'm dead and buried, Oh,
Susanna, don't you cry.

MEXICALI SALLY

Ingredients

1 lb. lean ground beef, browned
    ahead of time
½ onion, diced
1 (15 oz.) can chili beans, partially drained
Tortilla chips
3 C. shredded lettuce
2 tomatoes, chopped
2 C. Mexican blend shredded cheese
Taco sauce

Directions

Combine precooked ground beef and onion in skillet and set on hot coals; cook until onion is tender, stirring several times. Add beans and cook until heated through. To serve four, break up a handful of chips on each plate and spoon an equal portion of meat mixture over chips. Top with lettuce, tomatoes, cheese and taco sauce as desired.

BAKED BEANS & SAUSAGE

1 (8 oz.) pkg. smoked sausage
    links, sliced ½" thick
1½ C. chopped onions
¾ C. barbecue sauce
2 T. syrup
2 T. apple cider vinegar
1 (16 oz.) can red kidney beans, rinsed
1 (16 oz.) can pinto beans, rinsed
1 (16 oz.) can black beans, rinsed

Place grilling grate over campfire. Place sausage slices in a cast iron skillet and place skillet over heat. Cook sausage for 3 minutes on each side or until evenly browned. Remove sausage slices to a plate. Add chopped onions to skillet and cook until softened. Add barbecue sauce, syrup, apple cider vinegar and a little water. Bring mixture to a boil. Open all cans and add rinsed kidney beans, pinto beans and black beans to skillet. Return sausage slices to skillet. Mix well and cover skillet with lid. Heat, stirring occasionally, for about 15 minutes.

OLD-FASHIONED BEEF STEW

Ingredients

1 lb. beef stew meat, cubed
5 potatoes, cubed
1 C. baby-cut carrots
1 C. sliced celery
1 onion, chopped
½ C. whole kernel corn, optional
1 (1.5 oz.) pkg. beef stew seasoning mix
1 (.75 to .9 oz.) pkg. brown or
    mushroom gravy mix
Salt and pepper to taste

Directions

Set skillet on hot coals; add meat and enough water to cover. Bring to a simmer, cover with foil and cook for about 1 hour, checking frequently and adding more water if necessary. Add vegetables, cover and cook for 45 minutes or until tender. Stir in seasoning mix and gravy mix, adding water as needed to reach desired consistency; cook until heated through. Season with salt and pepper. Scoop into bowls to serve a group.

BASIC MULLIGAN STEW

Ingredients
1 lb. lean ground beef
1 onion, chopped
1 (14 oz.) can green beans
1 (15 oz.) can butter beans
1 (15 oz.) can sliced or diced potatoes
1 (14.5 oz.) can sliced carrots or diced carrots and peas
½ tsp. hot sauce
1 (14.5 oz.) can beef broth
1 (14.5 oz.) can diced Italian or plain tomatoes
1 (10.7 oz.) can tomato soup
Salt and pepper to taste

Directions
Before you leave home, cook ground beef and onion in a skillet until browned and tender; discard fat. Transfer to an airtight container and refrigerate or freeze until your trip.

Set skillet on a grate or trivet over hot coals or directly in medium coals; place precooked beef mixture in the skillet. Add undrained cans of green beans, butter beans, potatoes and carrots. Stir in hot sauce, broth, tomatoes and soup until blended. Season with salt and pepper. Cook until simmering and heated through, 20 to 30 minutes. Serves a bunch of hooligans.

Spice It Up: Start the stew with only the precooked ground beef mixture in the pot. Add a 1-ounce package of taco seasoning, one can each of pinto beans, mexicorn and stewed tomatoes. Mix together and bring to a simmer. Serve with corn chips.

Ham It Up: Make the stew as directed but in place of the precooked ground beef and beef broth, use chunks of ham and 2 cups water. Toss in ½ cup barley or lentils.

FIRESIDE FONDUE

Makes 6 to 8 servings
2 C. shredded Swiss cheese
2 T. flour
¼ tsp. paprika
1 (10¾ oz.) can cream of mushroom or broccoli soup
½ C. beer or white wine

Place grilling grate over campfire. Place shredded Swiss cheese, flour, paprika, cream of mushroom soup and beer in a cast iron skillet and place skillet over heat. Cook fondue, stirring frequently, until cheese is melted and mixture is heated throughout. Serve fondue with fresh veggies, crusty bread or crackers.

KAYAK TUNA MAC

Makes 2 servings

2 pkgs. Kraft Easy Mac
1 (6 oz.) can tuna in water, drained
1 (8½ oz.) can green peas, drained

Place grilling grate over campfire. Place 1¼ cups water in a cast iron skillet and place skillet over heat. Bring water to a boil and add noodles from Easy Mac packets. Boil noodles for 3 minutes. Remove skillet from heat and pour out excess water, leaving a little water in the skillet. Add cheese sauce packets, drained tuna and drained peas. Mix well. Return skillet to heat until mixture is heated throughout.

WILD & SLOPPY JOES

Makes 8 servings

2 lbs. ground beef
1 C. chopped celery
½ C. chopped onions
1 (10¾ oz.) can tomato soup
¼ C. ketchup
1 T. white vinegar
¼ C. brown sugar
1½ tsp. Worcestershire sauce
½ tsp. salt
¼ tsp. garlic powder
8 hamburger buns

Place grilling grate over campfire. Place ground beef in a cast iron skillet and place skillet over heat. Cook ground beef until evenly browned. Add chopped celery and chopped onions. Cook until celery and onions are tender and drain grease from skillet. Add tomato soup, ketchup, white vinegar, brown sugar and Worcestershire sauce. Mix well and season with salt and garlic powder. Let mixture simmer, stirring frequently, until heated throughout. Spoon mixture onto hamburger buns.

Quick Tip:

Chop onions and celery at home and pack in an airtight container. Place in cooler until ready to prepare recipe. Can also pack brown sugar, salt and garlic powder in a ziplock bag.

BEER-BATTERED FISH

Makes 8 servings

½ C. vegetable oil
1 C. beer
2 lbs. trout filets
1 C. Bisquick baking mix

Place grilling grate over campfire. Place vegetable oil in a cast iron skillet and place skillet over heat. In a medium bowl, combine Bisquick baking mix and beer. Mix well. Dip fish filets in batter. Using a pair of tongs, remove fish from batter and shake off excess. Place battered fish in hot oil in skillet. Fry fish until golden brown, about 3 to 4 minutes on each side.

COWBOY CASSEROLE

Makes 5 servings

½ lb. bacon
1 lb. ground beef
1 small onion, chopped
2 (15 oz.) cans pork n' beans
⅓ C. barbecue sauce
1 tube of 10 refrigerated biscuits

Place grilling grate over campfire. Place bacon in a cast iron skillet and place skillet over heat. Cook bacon to desired crispness and remove from skillet to paper towels. When bacon has drained, crumble and set aside. Add ground beef and chopped onions to skillet and cook until ground beef is evenly browned and onions are tender. Drain grease from skillet and add crumbled bacon, pork n' beans and barbecue sauce. Bring mixture to a low boil. Separate tube into individual biscuits and place biscuits over ingredients in skillet. Cover skillet and let simmer for about 10 minutes, or until biscuits are golden brown. Place two biscuits on each plate and spoon casserole over biscuits.

CHICKEN FAJITAS

Makes 6 servings

3 boneless skinless chicken breast halves
1 clove garlic, halved
1 medium green or red bell
  pepper, cut into strips
½ red onion, cut into strips
1½ C. shredded Cheddar cheese
6 flour tortillas
Salsa

Place grilling grate over campfire. Rub both sides of each chicken breast with garlic halves. Place chicken breasts in a cast iron skillet and place skillet over heat. Cook until chicken is heated throughout. Remove chicken to a plate and cut into strips. Add green or red pepper strips and onions to skillet and cook until softened. Return chicken to skillet. Spoon ¼ cup shredded Cheddar cheese and some salsa into the center of each tortilla. Fill each tortilla with some of the chicken, peppers and onions mixture. Fold tortillas to enclose mixture.

WALKING TACOS

Makes 4 serving

1 lb. prepared taco meat
Shredded lettuce
½ C. shredded Cheddar cheese
Chopped tomatoes
Sour cream
4 individual size bags Doritos

Place grilling grate over campfire. Place prepared taco meat in a cast iron skillet and place skillet over heat. Cook until taco meat is heated throughout. Open bags of Doritos and lightly crush the chips. Spoon heated taco meat into bags and top with shredded Cheddar cheese, shredded lettuce, chopped tomatoes and sour cream. Eat walking tacos with a fork right from the bag.

Quick Tip:

Prepare taco meat at home by browning 1 pound ground beef and mixing with ½ cup water and 1 envelope of taco seasoning. Pack in an airtight container and place in cooler until ready to prepare recipe.

SKILLET

Main Dishes

CREOLE CAMPOUT

Makes 4 serving

2 T. butter or margarine
1 medium onion, chopped
½ green bell pepper, chopped
½ C. chopped celery
2 T. flour
2 tsp. Cajun seasoning
1 (12 oz.) can tuna in water, drained
1 (15¼ oz.) can whole kernel corn

Place grilling grate over campfire. Place butter in a cast iron skillet and place skillet over heat. Cook until butter is melted and add chopped onions, chopped green bell pepper and chopped celery. Cook until vegetables are tender and add flour. Mix well and add Cajun seasoning, drained tuna and corn. Heat for 3 to 5 minutes, stirring occasionally.

QUICK & EASY TOMATO CASSEROLE

Makes 4 to 6 servings

1 T. vegetable oil
1 lb. ground beef
1 small onion, chopped
1 (14½ oz.) can stewed tomatoes in juice
1 (15 oz.) can whole kernel corn, drained

Place grilling grate over campfire. Place vegetable oil in a cast iron skillet and place skillet over heat. Add ground beef and cook until evenly browned. Add chopped onions and cook until onions are tender. Add stewed tomatoes in juice and drained corn. Cook until mixture is heated throughout. Spoon into bowls.

BEANS & TEXAS TOAST

Makes 4 servings

1 lb. ground beef
1 (15 oz.) can pork n' beans
4 slices Texas Toast
Butter
Garlic salt

Place grilling grate over campfire. Place ground beef in a cast iron skillet and place skillet over heat. Cook until ground beef is completely browned and cooked throughout. Add pork n' beans and mix well. Cook until mixture is heated throughout. Meanwhile, spread butter over both sides of each slice of bread and toast over camping stove or campfire. When toast is lightly browned, remove from heat and sprinkle with garlic salt. Spoon ground beef mixture into bowls and eat with toast on the side.

HUNGRY MAN'S POLISH SAUSAGE DINNER

Makes 2 to 4 servings

2 T. vegetable oil
1 pkg. Polish sausage
2 potatoes, peeled and chopped
2 sweet potatoes, peeled and chopped
1 large onion, chopped
1 green bell pepper, diced
1 red bell pepper, diced
1 yellow squash, chopped

Place grilling grate over campfire. Place vegetable oil in an extra large cast iron skillet and place skillet over heat. Add Polish sausage, chopped potatoes, chopped sweet potatoes, chopped onions, diced green and red bell peppers and chopped yellow squash. Cook sausage and vegetables until heated throughout. Remove sausages to a plate and cut into pieces. Return sausages to skillet and cook for an additional minute.

Quick Tip:
Prepare Polish sausage at home and chop into pieces. Pack in an airtight container and place in cooler until ready to prepare recipe.

PORK CHOP DINNER

Makes 2 servings

2 pork chops
2 potatoes, peeled and chopped
1 onion, chopped
1 small head cabbage, shredded
1 (10¾ oz.) can cream of mushroom soup

Place grilling grate over campfire. Place pork chops in a cast iron skillet and place skillet over heat. Cook pork chops until browned on both sides, turning once. Add chopped potatoes and chopped onions to skillet and sautéed until browned. Add shredded cabbage and cream of mushroom soup. Fill empty soup can with water and add to skillet. Mix slightly. Add lid to skillet and cook over heat for about 20 minutes, until potatoes are tender and mixture is heated throughout.

JACKED-UP CORN CAKES

Makes 12 cakes

8 bacon strips, diced
⅓ C. onion, finely chopped
1 C. flour
2 tsp. dried chives
1 tsp. baking powder
½ tsp. salt
⅛ tsp. cayenne pepper
⅔ C. milk, plus more as needed
1 egg, beaten
1 T. canola oil
1 C. whole kernel corn with
   diced peppers, drained
½ C. shredded Monterey Jack cheese
Maple syrup

Cook the bacon in a skillet on a rack over a cooking fire until just beginning to brown. Add the onion and cook until the bacon is crisp and the onion is tender, stirring often; drain and set aside.

In the meantime, mix the flour, chives, baking powder, salt and cayenne pepper. Add ⅔ cup milk, egg and oil, stirring until just moistened. Stir in the set-aside bacon mixture, the corn and the cheese. The batter will be thick (stir in a splash of milk to thin it slightly if you'd like).

Heat a little oil on a griddle. Use a ¼-cup measuring cup to pour batter into the hot oil and to spread batter slightly so the cakes aren't too thick. Cook a few minutes on each side until golden brown. Serve with syrup.

CAST IRON NACHOS

Ingredients

Tortilla chips, any variety
Chili con queso cheese sauce
Green onion, chopped
Tomato, chopped
Bell pepper, chopped
Taco meat
Sliced black olives
Your favorite shredded cheese
Sour cream
Salsa
Guacamole

Directions

In a large cast iron skillet, layer chips, cheese sauce, green onion, tomato, bell pepper, meat, olives and shredded cheese. Repeat layers. Set on a cooking rack over warm coals until cheese melts, covering with foil to help melt cheese, if needed.

Serve with sour cream, salsa, guacamole and any other favorites.

CORN HASH

Ingredients

5 strips bacon, cut into pieces
½ onion, chopped
Salt and pepper to taste
½ (14.5 oz.) can diced tomatoes
1 (15 oz.) can whole kernel corn
½ tsp. red pepper flakes, optional

Directions

Set skillet on hot coals and add bacon; cook until almost crisp, turning often. Add onion and fry for 2 minutes. Season lightly with salt and pepper. Add tomatoes and corn (with liquid). Bring to a simmer and cook until most of the liquid is gone, stirring frequently. Stir in pepper flakes, if desired, and serve hot. Makes about four servings.

WHITE BEAN BAKE

Ingredients
1½ T. butter
1 C. chopped onion
¼ C. maple syrup
2½ T. lemon juice
1 T. brown sugar
1½ tsp. dried crushed sage
2 T. ketchup
½ tsp. salt
¼ tsp. pepper
1 (15 oz.) can navy beans
1 (15 oz.) can garbanzo beans (chickpeas)
1 (15 oz.) can butter beans
Sour cream, optional
1 tomato, chopped, optional

Directions
Use a large skillet that will hold at least 6 cups. Set skillet on a grate or on medium-hot coals to melt butter. Add onion; cook and stir until tender and lightly browned. Stir in syrup, lemon juice, brown sugar, sage, ketchup, salt and pepper. Rinse and drain navy, garbanzo and butter beans; add beans to pot, stirring until coated in sauce.

Cover with foil and cook over medium coals, stirring occasionally, for 10 to 15 minutes or until heated through. Divide beans among six serving bowls and top with sour cream and tomato, if desired.

CAMPFIRE GREEN BEANS

Makes 6 servings
2 T. olive oil
1 Vidalia onion, chopped
1 clove garlic, minced
¼ C. slivered almonds
3 (14½ oz.) cans French cut
   green beans, drained
Salt and pepper to taste

Place grilling grate over campfire. Place olive oil, chopped onions, minced garlic and slivered almonds in a cast iron skillet and place skillet over heat. Sauté mixture until onions are tender, about 5 minutes. Add drained green beans to skillet and season with salt and pepper to taste. Cook until green beans are heated throughout.

Quick Tip:
Prepare entire recipe at home and pack green beans mixture in a ziplock bag and place in cooler. At campsite, place mixture in a cast iron skillet over stove or fire until heated throughout.

CALICO BEANS

Ingredients

½ C. ketchup
½ C. brown sugar
½ tsp. salt
1 tsp. dry mustard
2 tsp. vinegar
2 T. molasses
½ lb. lean ground beef, crumbled
½ lb. bacon, chopped
1 C. chopped onion
1 (15 oz.) can kidney beans
1 (15 oz.) can pork and beans
1 (15 oz.) can butter beans

Directions

Before you leave home, mix ketchup, brown sugar, salt, dry mustard, vinegar and molasses; store in an airtight container and chill. In a large skillet, cook ground beef, bacon and onion until browned; discard fat. Transfer to an airtight container and refrigerate or freeze until your trip. Place both containers in a cooler before hitting the road.

Set skillet on medium-hot coals. Add precooked beef mixture; stir until hot. Drain and add kidney beans. Stir in pork and beans, butter beans and prepared ketchup mixture from home. Cook for 30 minutes, stirring occasionally, until flavors are blended and mixture is hot.

BAKED BEANS

Ingredients

6 strips bacon
¼ C. ketchup
2 T. molasses
2 T. brown sugar
1 T. dried minced onion
2 T. yellow mustard
2 (15 oz.) cans pinto beans, drained
3 drops hot pepper sauce, or to taste

Directions

Cut bacon into 1" pieces and place in skillet. Set skillet on hot coals and cook bacon, stirring frequently, until crisp. Remove from heat. Add ketchup, molasses, brown sugar, onion and mustard to bacon and drippings in skillet; mix well. Set skillet on medium-hot coals and stir in beans and pepper sauce. Cook for 45 minutes, stirring frequently, until beans are hot and flavors are blended. Serves four campers.

RANCH-STYLE VEGGIES

Makes 4 servings

1 T. vegetable oil
1 (.4 oz.) env. Ranch dressing mix
2 medium carrots, peeled and thinly sliced
2 medium yellow squash, thinly sliced
2 medium zucchini, thinly sliced

Place grilling grate over campfire. Place vegetable oil and Ranch dressing mix in a cast iron skillet and place skillet over heat. Mix well and add sliced carrots. Cook carrots for 4 to 5 minutes, until tender but crisp. Add squash and zucchini and cook for an additional 4 to 5 minutes, until vegetables are tender. Remove vegetables from skillet with a slotted spoon.

BANANA BROWNIES

Ingredients

2 egg whites, lightly beaten
⅓ C. buttermilk
1 tsp. vanilla extract
1 C. semi-sweet chocolate chips
⅔ C. flour
⅔ C. sugar
⅓ C. nonfat dry milk
¼ C. unsweetened cocoa powder
1 tsp. ground cinnamon
½ tsp. baking soda
¼ tsp. salt
1 banana, sliced
Powdered sugar

Directions

Grease skillet with nonstick cooking spray and set aside. In a bowl, mix egg whites, buttermilk and vanilla; set aside. In another bowl, mix chocolate chips, flour, sugar, dry milk, cocoa powder, cinnamon, baking soda and salt; make a well in the center. Add egg mixture; stir until combined. Spread batter in prepared skillet. Arrange banana slices on top.

Cover skillet tightly with foil. Place on a grate over medium-low coals or embers and cook for 25 to 30 minutes or until edges start to pull away from skillet. Cool 30 minutes; cut into 12 pieces. Sprinkle with powdered sugar before serving.

GRILLED BERRY CRUMBLE

Ingredients

5 C. assorted fresh or frozen berries
¼ C. sugar
¾ C. brown sugar, divided
2 T. plus ¼ C. flour, divided
½ C. quick-cooking oats
¼ tsp. ground nutmeg
¼ tsp. ground cinnamon
¼ C. butter

Directions

Set a skillet on medium-hot coals. Add berries, sugar, ¼ cup brown sugar and 2 tablespoons flour. Cook and stir until thickened and bubbly. In a bowl, combine oats, remaining ½ cup brown sugar and ¼ cup flour, nutmeg and cinnamon. Cut in butter until crumbly. Sprinkle oat topping over fruit mixture.

Cover skillet tightly with foil and place on a grate over medium-hot coals. Cook for 30 to 40 minutes, rotating pan several times for even heat. Serves about eight.

Quick Crumble

Use canned pie filling in place of prepared berry mixture.

FRUITY GRILL

Ingredients

1 C. fresh or canned pineapple chunks
1 or 2 bananas, peeled and sliced
1 C. sliced fresh strawberries
1 C. pitted fresh cherries
16 regular marshmallows

Directions

Grease skillet lightly with nonstick cooking spray. Combine pineapple, bananas, strawberries and cherries in skillet, stirring to mix. Arrange marshmallows on top. Cover skillet with foil and place on medium-hot coals for 15 minutes or until marshmallows begin to melt and fruit is hot. Spoon into bowls to satisfy the sweet tooth of four to six people.

FRY BROWNIES

Ingredients

1 C. flour
¼ C. unsweetened cocoa powder
¾ C. sugar
1 tsp. baking powder
¼ tsp. salt
2 T. nonfat dry milk
½ C. mini semi-sweet chocolate chips
¼ C. walnuts, optional
4 T. vegetable oil, divided

Directions

Before leaving home, stir together flour, cocoa powder, sugar, baking powder, salt and dry milk. Add chocolate chips and walnuts, if desired. Divide mixture among six zippered plastic bags, placing ½ cup of mix in each bag. Each bag will make 1 serving.

Place skillet over medium-low coals or embers. To one bag of prepared brownie mix, add 1 teaspoon vegetable oil and 1½ tablespoons water; knead mixture in bag until blended. Heat 1 teaspoon oil in skillet. Cut off a large piece from one corner of plastic bag and squeeze spoon-sized mounds of brownie batter into hot skillet. Cook until bottoms are browned and tops are no longer shiny. Flip brownies over, flatten as needed and cook until other side is lightly browned. Let cool before serving.

CHOCOLATE COINS

Ingredients

1 C. pancake mix
1 pkg. hot chocolate mix
2 T. pecan chips
Water
Powdered sugar
Chocolate syrup or melted
  chocolate, optional

Directions

Spray skillet generously with nonstick cooking spray and place over medium coals. In a bowl, combine pancake mix, chocolate mix and pecans with enough water to make a batter. When a drop of water in the skillet sizzles, drop small amounts of batter into skillet to make several coin-size pancakes. These will cook quickly. Turn over when the edges begin to appear set. Remove from skillet and dust with powdered sugar. Enjoy warm or cold. Chocoholics will enjoy dipping these "coins" into chocolate syrup or melted chocolate.

Quick Tip:

Add a spoonful or two of sugar to leftover pancake batter and fry coin-size pancakes. Sprinkle powdered sugar between each one and wrap batch in foil. Store in cooler until desired. Serve coins warm or cold with peanut butter, melted chocolate or warmed fruit preserves.

BURST VANILLA APPLES

Ingredients

4 large baking apples
  (Jonathans or Granny Smiths)
¼ C. granulated sugar
5 T. water
1 (2" length) vanilla pod (bean), split in two

Directions

Peel, core and quarter the apples. Place them in a single layer in a large, heavy skillet. Split the vanilla bean lengthwise. Using the tip of a small knife, scrape the vanilla seeds over the apples. Place the vanilla sections among the apples. Sprinkle sugar over the top. Pour the water over the top of the apple quarters.

Place skillet over medium heat, and cook, uncovered, until the liquid start to simmer. Then raise the skillet by putting it on a grate or rack so that the heat under the skillet is reduced to low. Cover tightly with foil, and cook (shaking the skillet gently from time to time) for approximately 20 to 25 minutes until the apple quarters are soft and on the verge of collapse (but still hold their form). Remove from heat and serve immediately, pouring juices from the skillet over the apples.

Makes four to six servings.

CAST IRON COOKIE

Serves a crowd

1 C. butter, softened
1 C. brown sugar
1 C. sugar
2 eggs
1 T. vanilla
3 C. flour
¾ tsp. baking soda
1 tsp. sea salt
½ C. quick-cooking oats
1½ C. baking chips (we used a combination of semi-sweet chocolate chunks, semi-sweet mini chips, and white chips)

Preheat the grill on low heat. In a big bowl, mix butter, brown sugar and sugar until light and fluffy; beat in eggs and vanilla. Slowly add flour, baking soda, sea salt and quick-cooking oats, mixing until blended. Stir in baking chips.

Grease a 12" cast iron skillet with shortening and press the dough into it. Set on the grill, close the lid and cook until golden brown and done in the middle, rotating the pan occasionally (this could take 25 minutes or longer, depending on the heat of your grill—don't rush it). Cool slightly before cutting.

If you're cooking away from home, mix the dough ahead of time and tote it in the cooler. (Don't eat all the dough on the way though!)

DUTCH OVEN

Dutch ovens are a versatile piece of cooking equipment. You can boil, fry, bake, and anything in-between. The legs allow the oven to stand a bit above hot coals, and a rim around the lid allows hot coals to stay in place on top of the oven—so heat comes from above and below.

A real Dutch oven is a great way to cook on a campfire, but it's heavy and hard to carry around. Here's how to make one that can be thrown away.

Brass Fasteners

Binder Clips

Need

- 3 (9") disposable aluminum foil pie pans
- Push pin
- 2 brass paper fasteners
- 3 metal clips or strips of heavy-duty foil

Directions

Place the bottoms of two pie pans together, edges even. With push pin, make a starter hole on each side of the center point, going through both pans and placing holes about 2" apart. Push paper fasteners through the holes; open prongs and flatten securely. (The pie pan with the round fastener heads will be the lid of your Dutch oven and the attached pan with the prongs will be on top to hold hot coals during cooking.)

To use, place food in remaining pie pan and set the lid on top. Seal edges with metal clips or strips of crimped foil.

FRUIT-FILLED BREAKFAST BREAD

Makes 8 servings

4 C. Bisquick baking mix
4 tsp. cinnamon
1 C. golden raisins
½ C. chopped dried apples
1 C. shredded coconut
1 C. chopped almonds
1 C. sugar
½ (16 oz.) pkg. Eggbeaters dry
    scrambled egg mix
4 C. shredded carrots
1 C. vegetable oil
2 tsp. vanilla, optional
1¼ C. water

Build a campfire using briquettes and dig a hole in the coals for the Dutch oven. In a large bowl, combine baking mix, cinnamon, golden raisins, chopped dried apples, shredded coconut, chopped almonds, sugar and dry scrambled egg mix. Add shredded carrots, vegetable oil, vanilla and water to dry mixture and mix until a batter forms. Lightly oil Dutch oven and pour batter into Dutch oven. Set Dutch oven in hole. Place lid on Dutch oven and set 15 to 20 briquettes on lid. Bake bread for 25 to 35 minutes, checking after 15 minutes.

BREAKFAST PIZZA

Makes 6 to 8 servings

1 lb. sausage
1 (8 oz.) pkg. refrigerated crescent rolls
3 T. diced red bell peppers
3 T. diced green bell peppers
1 C. frozen hash browns, thawed
1 green onion, sliced
1 C. shredded Cheddar cheese
3 eggs, beaten
3 T. milk
½ tsp. salt
1 tsp. pepper
3 T. grated Parmesan cheese

Build a campfire using briquettes and dig a hole in the coals for the Dutch oven. Place sausage in a 12" Dutch oven and set Dutch oven in hole. Cook sausage for 5 to 10 minutes, until evenly browned. Drain pot of grease and transfer sausage to a separate plate. If using links, chop sausage links into pieces. Unroll crescent rolls and line the bottom of Dutch oven with crescent rolls. Sprinkle sausage, diced bell peppers, hash browns, sliced green onions and shredded Cheddar cheese over crescent rolls. In a medium bowl, combine eggs, milk, salt and pepper. Pour mixture evenly over ingredients in Dutch oven. Sprinkle grated Parmesan cheese over egg mixture. Place lid on Dutch oven and set 8 to 10 briquettes on lid. Bake breakfast pizza for 20 to 30 minutes or until eggs are set.

HAM & CABBAGE STEW

Ingredients

1 meaty ham bone
1 (14 oz.) pkg. kielbasa or
   smoked sausage, sliced
1 head green cabbage, chopped
3 carrots, sliced
3 potatoes, diced
1 onion, chopped
3 cloves garlic, minced
1 (14.5 oz.) can diced tomatoes
1 (15 oz.) can green beans
1 (15 oz.) can whole kernel corn
1 green bell pepper, seeded, chopped
1 zucchini, cut into chunks
Salt and pepper to taste

Directions

Set pot on hot coals. Place ham bone and sausage in Dutch oven. Add cabbage, carrots, potatoes, onion, garlic, tomatoes, green beans and corn (with juice), bell pepper and zucchini. Add 4 cups water and season with salt and pepper. Bring mixture to a boil. Move to medium coals and let stew simmer for 1 to 2 hours or until vegetables are tender and flavors are well blended. Ladle soup directly into bowls to serve a crowd.

FIVE-CAN SOUP

Makes 6 servings

1 (14½ oz.) can diced tomatoes
1 (8½ oz.) can mixed vegetables
1 (15 oz.) can white corn, drained
1 (15 oz.) can black beans,
   rinsed and drained
1 (10½ oz.) can minestrone soup

Build a campfire using briquettes and set up tripod for a Dutch oven. Open all cans and place diced tomatoes in juice, mixed vegetables in juice, drained corn, drained black beans and minestrone soup in Dutch oven. Hang Dutch oven over heat. Let soup heat for about 20 minutes, stirring occasionally.

FIESTA CHICKEN SOUP

Makes 10 to 12 servings
- 1 (32 oz.) can chicken broth
- 2 (14½ oz.) cans whole kernel corn, undrained
- 1 (14 to 16 oz.) can Ranch style beans
- 1 (10 oz.) can diced tomatoes with green chilies
- 2 chicken bouillon cubes
- 1 (10 oz.) can white chunk chicken, drained
- 1 (8 oz.) box Velveeta light cheese

Build a campfire using briquettes and set up tripod for a Dutch oven. Open all cans and place chicken broth, corn in juice, Ranch style beans, diced tomatoes with green chilies, chicken bouillon cubes and drained white chunk chicken in Dutch oven. Hang Dutch oven over heat. Cook mixture, stirring occasionally, until heated throughout. Cut Velveeta cheese into cubes. Add cheese cubes to soup and stir until cheese is melted.

HOBO STEW

Makes 4 servings
- 1 lb. ground beef
- 1 large onion, chopped
- 1 (28 oz.) can baked beans
- 1 large can water

Build a campfire using briquettes and set up tripod for a Dutch oven. Place ground beef in Dutch oven and hang Dutch oven over heat. Cook ground beef for about 5 minutes, until evenly browned. Drain pot of grease and add chopped onions and baked beans. Fill empty baked beans can with water and add to pot. Cook until stew is heated throughout.

Quick Tip:

"Sticking can be one of the biggest issues to overcome when cooking in camp ovens. To prevent sticking, warm [it] slightly to get rid of any moisture and then wipe a small bit of oil around [it] with a plastic bag." (from *Canoe Camping* by Mark Scriver)

BIG POND SOUP

Makes 24 servings

1 lb. lean ground beef
1 (15 oz.) can carrots, drained
1 (15¼ oz.) can whole kernel corn
1 (15 oz.) can green beans
1 (15 oz.) can peas
1 (15 oz.) can sliced potatoes
1 (15 oz.) can mixed vegetables
1 (10 oz.) can asparagus
1 (46 oz.) can tomato juice
1 medium head cabbage, chopped
½ tsp. garlic powder
1 tsp. onion powder
Salt and pepper to taste

Build a campfire using briquettes and set up tripod for a Dutch oven. Place ground beef in Dutch oven and hang Dutch oven over heat. Cook ground beef until evenly browned. Drain pot and crumble the ground beef, leaving ground beef in the pot. Open all of the cans and drain liquid only from the carrots. Add drained carrots, corn in juice, green beans in juice, peas in juice, sliced potatoes in juice, mixed vegetables in juice, asparagus in juice, tomato juice and chopped cabbage to the Dutch oven. Season with garlic powder and onion powder. Cook soup until heated throughout and cabbage is tender. Add salt and pepper to taste.

STARRY NIGHT CHILI

Makes 12 servings

3 lbs. ground beef
3 onions, chopped
10 cloves garlic, minced
3 (15 oz.) cans pork n' beans
3 (15 oz.) cans kidney beans, drained
1 (14½ oz.) can stewed tomatoes
3 T. chili powder
1 (12 oz.) can beer
Salt and pepper to taste

Build a campfire using briquettes and set up tripod for a Dutch oven. Place ground beef in Dutch oven and hang Dutch oven over heat. Cook ground beef for about 5 minutes, until evenly browned. Add chopped onions and minced garlic and sauté for an additional 5 to 10 minutes. Add pork n' beans, drained kidney beans, stewed tomatoes in juice, chili powder and beer. Reduce heat to low or move pot to outer edge of grate. Cover pot and let simmer for 60 minutes, stirring occasionally. Season with salt and pepper to taste.

PASTA DOGS

Makes 10 servings
2 (6 oz.) pkgs. spaghetti pasta
1 pkg. hot dogs
1 (28 oz.) jar pasta sauce

Build a campfire using briquettes and dig a hole in the coals for the Dutch oven. Fill Dutch oven with water and set Dutch oven in hole. Add spaghetti to pot and bring to a boil. Meanwhile, cut hot dogs into bite-size pieces. When spaghetti is tender, drain Dutch oven and return cooked spaghetti to the pot. Add pasta sauce and hot dog pieces. Mix well and cook over heat until hot dogs are heated throughout.

ONE-POT LASAGNA

Makes 12 servings
2 lbs. lasagna noodles
5 lbs. ground beef
3 lbs. spicy ground sausage
2 (16 oz.) containers cottage cheese
6 eggs
3 (8 oz.) pkgs. shredded mozzarella cheese
1 (28 oz.) jar pasta sauce

Build a campfire using briquettes and dig a hole in the coals for the Dutch oven. Fill a 14" Dutch oven with water and set Dutch oven in hole. Bring water to a boil and add lasagna noodles. Cook until noodles are tender and transfer noodles to a plate. Drain pot. Place ground beef and spicy ground sausage in Dutch oven. Cook ground beef and sausage for 5 to 10 minutes, until evenly browned. Drain pot of grease and transfer ground beef and sausage to a separate plate. In a medium bowl, combine cottage cheese and eggs. Build lasagna by placing layers of meat, cottage cheese mixture, shredded mozzarella cheese and noodles in Dutch oven. Repeat layers until pot is almost full. Pour spaghetti sauce over lasagna and sprinkle remaining shredded cheese on top. Place lid on Dutch oven and set 10 to 12 briquettes on lid. Cook over heat for about 45 minutes.

Quick Tip:
Cook ground beef and ground sausage at home and pack in an airtight container. Place in cooler until ready to prepare recipe.

CAMPSKETTI

Makes 10 servings

½ lb. lean ground beef
1 medium onion, chopped
1 (4 oz.) can mushrooms, drained, optional
1 (14 oz.) can chicken broth
1 (6 oz.) can tomato paste
1¾ C. water
¼ tsp. pepper
½ tsp. dried basil
1 tsp. dried oregano
⅛ tsp. garlic powder
1 (6 oz.) pkg. spaghetti pasta, broken

Build a campfire using briquettes and dig a hole in the coals for the Dutch oven. Place ground beef and chopped onions in Dutch oven and set Dutch oven in hole. Cook ground beef and onions for about 5 minutes, until evenly browned. Drain pot of grease and add drained mushrooms, chicken broth, tomato paste, water, pepper, basil, oregano and garlic powder. Bring mixture to a boil and add broken spaghetti. Cook, stirring frequently, until spaghetti is tender, about 20 minutes.

Quick Tip:
Prepare seasoning packet at home by combining pepper, dried basil, dried oregano and garlic powder in a ziplock bag.

COCA-COLA CHICKEN

Makes 8 servings

8 boneless skinless chicken breast halves
1 (12 oz.) can Coca-Cola
1½ C. ketchup
1 yellow onion, diced
3 cloves garlic, minced
1 T. chili powder

Build a campfire using briquettes and dig a hole in the coals for the Dutch oven. Place chicken breast halves in a 12" Dutch oven. Set Dutch oven in hole. In a large bowl, combine Coca-Cola, ketchup, diced yellow onion, minced garlic and chili powder. Mix well and pour mixture over chicken. Place lid on Dutch oven and set 14 to 16 briquettes on lid. Bake chicken for 60 to 75 minutes or until chicken is cooked throughout.

Main Dishes

DUTCH OVEN

CHICKEN POT PIE

Makes 8 servings

2 large chicken breasts, cooked and cubed
2 (8½ oz.) cans mixed vegetables
   with potatoes
1 (10¾ oz.) can cream of chicken soup
1 (10¾ oz.) can cream of mushroom soup
1 tube of 10 refrigerated biscuits

Build a campfire using briquettes and dig a hole in the coals for the Dutch oven. Place chicken, mixed vegetables in juice, cream of chicken soup and cream of mushroom soup in Dutch oven and set Dutch oven in hole. Mix well and heat mixture, being careful not to boil. When mixture is warmed throughout, place biscuits on top of chicken mixture. Place lid on Dutch oven and set 14 to 16 briquettes on lid. Heat mixture with biscuits for 15 to 30 minutes, checking biscuits after 15 minutes.

Quick Tip:

Prepare chicken breasts at home and cut into cubes. Pack in an airtight container and place in cooler until ready to prepare recipe.

Main Dishes

DUTCH OVEN

CAMPOUT CORNBREAD

Makes 10 to 12 servings

1 C. butter, melted
4 eggs, beaten
3 C. milk
2 C. sugar
2 C. cornmeal
3 C. flour
4 tsp. baking powder
1 tsp. salt

Build a campfire using briquettes and dig a hole in the coals for the Dutch oven. In a large bowl, combine melted butter, eggs and milk. Add sugar, cornmeal, flour, baking powder and salt. Lightly grease a 12" Dutch oven and spoon cornbread mixture into pot. Set Dutch oven in hole. Place lid on Dutch oven and set 14 to 16 briquettes on lid. Bake for 45 minutes or until cornbread is golden brown.

Quick Tip:

Prepare dry mix at home by combining sugar, cornmeal, flour, baking powder and salt. Pack in an airtight container until ready to prepare recipe.

FIESTA TACO BAKE WITH CORNBREAD

Makes 6 servings

1 lb. lean ground beef
1 (11 oz.) can Mexican-style corn, drained
⅔ C. water
1 (1 oz.) pkg. taco seasoning
1¼ C. shredded Cheddar cheese,
   plus more for sprinkling
¾ C. yellow cornmeal
¼ C. flour
2 T. sugar
2 tsp. baking powder
¾ tsp. salt
1 C. evaporated milk
1 egg
Tomatoes, chopped

Cook the ground beef in a 10" Dutch oven over a spread of medium-hot coals until crumbly and cooked through. Press the meat with paper towels to absorb excess grease. Stir in the corn, water and taco seasoning. Cook 5 to 10 minutes or until mixture thickens, stirring often. Sprinkle with 1¼ cups cheese and move off the heat.

In a medium bowl, mix the cornmeal, flour, sugar, baking powder and salt. In another bowl, whisk together evaporated milk and egg; add to cornmeal mixture and stir until blended. Spread over the ingredients in Dutch oven and cover with the lid. Set Dutch oven on a ring of 8 hot coals and arrange about 10 more hot coals on the lid. Bake 12 to 15 minutes or until cornbread tests done with a toothpick. Sprinkle with more cheese and tomatoes before serving.

Quick Tip:

Prep ahead: Before leaving home, combine the dry ingredients for the cornbread in an airtight bowl and mix the evaporated milk and egg in another airtight container. It makes mixing the batter at a campsite super fast and easy.

STUFFED SAUSAGE BOATS

Makes 4 servings

1 (14 oz.) kielbasa sausage
1 (24 oz.) tub refrigerated mashed
   potatoes (or use 3 C. homemade)
2 T. green onion, chopped
2 tsp. prepared yellow mustard
Black pepper, to taste
Paprika

Spritz a 10" or 12" Dutch oven with cooking spray. Cut kielbasa sausage into four equal pieces and slice each one lengthwise without cutting through the bottom; carefully lay each piece open like a book. Place in the Dutch oven, cut sides up.

In a bowl, stir together mashed potatoes, green onion, yellow mustard and black pepper; spoon evenly over the sausages and sprinkle with paprika.

Cover the Dutch oven and set it on a layer of hot coals for 15 to 20 minutes or until sausage sizzles and everything is hot. Sprinkle shredded cheddar cheese over each sausage boat; cover and heat just until cheese melts. Remove boats and top with cooked crumbled bacon and more green onion.

Desserts

DUTCH OVEN

THE CAMPER'S COBBLER

Makes 4 servings

1 (29 oz.) can sliced peaches in syrup
1 (30 oz.) can fruit cocktail in syrup
1 (20 oz.) can crushed pineapple in juice
½ C. instant tapioca
1 (18 oz.) pkg. white cake mix
1 C. brown sugar
½ C. butter or margarine

Build a campfire using briquettes and dig a hole in the coals for the Dutch oven. Line Dutch oven with aluminum foil. Open all cans and add sliced peaches in syrup, fruit cocktail in syrup, crushed pineapple in juice and instant tapioca to Dutch oven. Set Dutch oven in hole. Sprinkle white cake mix over fruit and tapioca and sprinkle brown sugar over cake mix. Dab pieces of butter over brown sugar. Place lid on Dutch oven and set 14 to 16 briquettes on lid. Bake cobbler for 45 to 60 minutes. The cobbler is done when cake mix has absorbed the juices and is no longer dry.

BLACK FOREST COBBLER

Makes 4 to 6 servings

1 (12 oz.) can cherry pie filling
1 (18 oz.) pkg. chocolate cake mix
¼ C. chopped walnuts
1 or 2 Hershey's chocolate bars
1 can soda (cherry or lemon-lime)

Build a campfire using briquettes and dig a hole in the coals for the Dutch oven. Add cherry pie filling to Dutch oven and pour chocolate cake mix over cherry filling. Pour half of the can of soda on top of the cake mix, and stir the soda into the cake mix, being careful not to mix it in with the pie filling. Add chopped walnuts. Break Hershey's bars in pieces and sprinkle over walnuts. Do not stir. Place lid over Dutch oven and set Dutch oven in hole. Cook for about 45 minutes.

FRUIT & RICE PUDDING

Makes 2 servings

¾ C. instant brown rice
1½ C. dried assorted fruit
½ C. evaporated milk
1 (8 oz.) can sweetened condensed milk
Pinch of nutmeg
Pinch of ground ginger
Pinch of brown sugar
Pinch of cinnamon

Build a campfire using briquettes and dig a hole in the coals for the Dutch oven. Add 2½ cups water to Dutch oven and bring to a boil. Set Dutch oven in hole and add instant brown rice and dried fruit. Cook until fruit is tender and rice is softened, about 8 to 10 minutes. Add evaporated milk, sweetened condensed milk, nutmeg, ground ginger, brown sugar and cinnamon. Mix well and heat for a few more minutes.

Quick Tip:

Prepare dry mix at home by combining evaporated milk, nutmeg, ground ginger, brown sugar and cinnamon. Pack mixture in a ziplock bag until ready to prepare recipe.

Your Personal Checklist for a Summer Camping Trip

- 1 pair boots for wet weather
- 1 pair sneakers
- 4 (or more) pair of socks (athletic sock weight)
- 4 (or more) sets underwear
- 2 long-sleeved shirts
- 2 long pants

- 1 lightweight windproof jacket
- 1 sweater or sweatshirt
- 1 rain suit or raincoat
- 1 hat with brim
- 1 set personal toilet articles, toothbrush, etc.
- 1 towel
- 1 swimming suit
- 2 bottles insect repellent

- 1 sleeping bag
- 1 foam or air mattress
- 2 large handkerchiefs
- 1 large flashlight with extra batteries
- 1 cup, metal or plastic, with handle
- 1 pocketknife
- 1 bag or pack to hold the above

(from *Master Guide Handbook to Outdoor Adventure Trips* by Gil Gilpatrick)

Desserts

DUTCH OVEN

CARAMEL APPLE CRISP

Desserts

DUTCH OVEN

Makes 16 servings

2 (12 oz.) cans apple pie filling
2 tsp. cinnamon
¾ tsp. nutmeg
¼ tsp. ground cloves
¾ tsp. salt
1 (12 oz.) jar caramel sauce
2 C. brown sugar
2 C. flour
1 C. instant oatmeal
½ C. chopped walnuts
1 C. butter, melted

Build a campfire using briquettes and dig a hole in the coals for the Dutch oven. Grease a 12" Dutch oven and add apple pie filling. Sprinkle cinnamon, nutmeg, ground cloves and salt over pie filling and mix well. Pour caramel sauce over apple mixture. In a medium bowl, combine brown sugar, flour, instant oatmeal, chopped walnuts and melted butter. Stir mixture with a fork until coarse crumbs form. Sprinkle topping evenly over apple mixture. Set Dutch oven in hole. Place lid on Dutch oven and set 10 to 12 briquettes on lid. Bake apple crisp for about 60 minutes.

Quick Tip:

Prepare dry mixes at home by combining cinnamon, nutmeg, ground cloves and salt. In a separate bowl, combine brown sugar, flour, instant oatmeal and chopped walnuts. Pack mixes in separate ziplock bags until ready to prepare recipe.

ON A GRATE

Grates are fantastic to use in campfire cooking. You may have the fortune to camp at a site with adjustable campfire grills set up; if not, grab a grill grate or sturdy cookie rack and set it on empty cans, bricks, or whatever else you can find that's steady. If desired, cover your grate with foil to prevent the loss of vittles into the flames.

Cleaning Your Grate or Grill Rack

1. While the grate is still hot, scrub it with a wire brush to loosen food debris.
2. Spread wet newspapers on the ground. Carefully remove hot grate and place it on newspapers, covering with more wet newspapers. Allow the grate to cool.
3. Meanwhile, spread dry newspapers on the ground nearby. When grate is cool enough to handle, wipe off debris as you remove the wet newspapers.
4. While wearing latex gloves and eye protection, spray commercial oven cleaner onto both sides of the grate, and follow product directions for standing time.
5. Scrub the grate with a wire brush and scouring pad to remove grime.
6. Rinse thoroughly with fresh water.
7. Dry grate with paper towels.
8. Before using grate again, rub it with a paper towel coated in oil.

STUFFED FRANKFURTERS

Makes 8 servings

8 frankfurters
1 (6 oz.) pkg. stuffing mix, prepared
8 slices bacon

Place grilling grate over campfire. Using a knife, cut a lengthwise slit in each frankfurter. Stuff frankfurters with prepared stuffing. Wrap one slice of bacon around each frankfurter, holding the stuffing inside. Secure with toothpicks. Place frankfurters over grill and cook until bacon reaches desired crispness and frankfurters reach desired doneness. Remove toothpicks before serving.

Quick Tip:
Prepare stuffing at home and pack in an airtight container. Place in cooler until ready to prepare recipe.

CHEESE-STUFFED BRATS

Makes 5 servings

5 fully cooked bratwurst
¼ C. shredded Monterey Jack cheese
2 green onions, thinly sliced
5 slices bacon
5 hot dog buns or French-style
    rolls, halved lengthwise
Ketchup, mustard and/or relish, optional

Place grilling grate over campfire. Using a knife, cut a lengthwise slit, about ½" deep, in each bratwurst. Stuff each bratwurst with some of the shredded Monterey Jack cheese and green onion slices. Wrap one slice of bacon around each bratwurst, holding the cheese inside. Secure with toothpicks. Place bratwurst, cheese side up, over grill and cook until bacon reaches desired crispness and bratwurst reach desired doneness, about 5 to 10 minutes. Remove toothpicks from bratwurst and place each bratwurst on 1 hot dog bun. If desired, garnish with ketchup, mustard and/or relish.

CARNE ASADA

Makes 4 servings

- 4 (¾" thick) beef rib eye steaks, trimmed
- 2 T. fresh lime juice
- 4 (6") flour tortillas
- 1 C. shredded Colby and Monterey Jack cheese, divided
- Salsa

Place grilling grate over campfire. Sprinkle half of the lime juice onto one side of each steak and rub into surface. Turn steaks and repeat with remaining lime juice. Wrap tortillas in aluminum foil. Place steaks on hot grate and grill for 12 to 15 minutes, turning once, or until steaks reach desired doneness. During last 5 minutes of cooking time, place aluminum-wrapped tortillas on outer edge of grate, turning once. Top each steak with ¼ cup shredded cheese and grill for an additional 1 or 2 minutes. Remove steaks from grill and top each steak with salsa. Serve steaks with heated tortillas on the side.

HONEY GARLIC PORK CHOPS

Makes 4 servings

- ¼ C. lemon juice
- ¼ C. honey
- 2 T. soy sauce
- 1 T. dry sherry
- 2 cloves garlic, minced
- 4 (4 oz.) boneless lean pork chops

In a heavy-duty ziplock bag, combine lemon juice, honey, soy sauce, dry sherry and minced garlic. Place pork chops in bag and seal. Let pork chops marinate in a cooler filled with ice for 4 hours or overnight. Place grilling grate over campfire. Remove pork chops from bag and place pork chops on hot grate. Grill pork chops for 12 to 15 minutes, turning once, until pork chops reach an internal temperature of 155°F to 160°F.

Quick Tip:
Prepare marinade at home and place pork chops in bag with marinade. Pack marinating pork chops in cooler with ice until ready to prepare recipe.

SALMON ON THE BARBIE

Makes 4 servings
- 4 salmon steaks, (¾" to 1" thick)
- 3 T. lemon juice
- 2 T. soy sauce
- Salt and pepper to taste
- ½ C. barbecue sauce

Place grilling grate over campfire. Rinse salmon steaks under running water and pat dry with paper towels. In a heavy-duty ziplock bag, combine lemon juice and soy sauce. Place salmon steaks in bag and let marinate for no more than 15 minutes. Remove salmon from bag and season lightly with salt and pepper. Place salmon steaks on hot grate and cook for 10 to 14 minutes. Halfway through grilling time, brush salmon steaks with barbecue sauce, turn and continue grilling. Salmon is done when it flakes easily with a fork. Remove salmon from grate and brush with additional barbecue sauce.

SOUTHWEST CHICKEN

Makes 4 servings
- 2 T. olive oil
- 1 clove garlic, pressed
- 1 tsp. chili powder
- 1 tsp. ground cumin
- 1 tsp. dried oregano
- ½ tsp. salt
- 1 lb. skinless boneless chicken breast halves or thighs

Place grilling grate over campfire. In a small bowl, combine olive oil, pressed garlic, chili powder, ground cumin, dried oregano and salt. Brush mixture over both sides of chicken breasts or thighs. Place chicken on hot grate and cook over grill for 8 to 10 minutes, turning once, until chicken is cooked throughout.

Quick Tip:
Prepare basting sauce at home and pack in an airtight container. Place in cooler until ready to prepare recipe.

BEER CAN CHICKEN

Makes 4 to 6 servings

1 (4 to 5 lbs.) whole chicken
¾ tsp. kosher salt
¾ tsp. sugar
¾ tsp. pepper
¾ tsp. paprika
1 (12 oz.) can beer

Place grilling grate over campfire. Remove and discard fat from inside the body cavity of the chicken. Remove giblets and rinse chicken, inside and out, under cool running water. Drain chicken and pat dry with paper towels. In a small bowl, combine kosher salt, sugar, pepper and paprika. Mix well. Sprinkle 1 tablespoon of the rub inside the body cavity and spread the remaining rub over the outside of the chicken. Open beer can and, using a can opener, poke 6 or 7 holes in the top of the can. Drink or pour out 1" of beer from the can. Holding the chicken upright, insert beer can into body cavity of chicken. Cover tips of the chicken legs with aluminum foil and stand chicken up on beer can over center of hot grate. Spread out legs of chicken to form a tripod.

Cook chicken until meat is tender, about 2 hours, and internal temperature of chicken reaches 160°F. Carefully remove can from chicken, being careful not to spill the hot beer. To serve, carve chicken from the bone.

Quick Tip:
Prepare seasoning rub at home and pack in an airtight container until ready to prepare recipe.

FIRESIDE PIZZA

Makes 4 to 6 servings

1 (13 or 14 oz.) tube prepared pizza crust
1 (14½ oz.) can pizza sauce
1 (8 oz.) pkg. shredded cheese, any kind
Pizza toppings, such as pepperoni slices,
    tomatoes, mushrooms, green peppers, etc.

Cover the grate with aluminum foil. Place grilling grate over campfire. Place prepared pizza crust on aluminum foil on grill. Top crust with pizza sauce, shredded cheese and pizza toppings of choice. Cook pizza until cheese is melted.

CLASSIC CHICKEN

Makes 6 servings

1 (3½ lbs.) whole frying chicken, quartered
¼ C. lemon juice
¼ C. olive oil
2 T. soy sauce
2 large cloves garlic, minced
½ tsp. sugar
½ tsp. ground cumin
¼ tsp. pepper

Rinse chicken under running water and pat dry with paper towels. In a heavy-duty extra large ziplock bag combine lemon juice, olive oil, soy sauce, minced garlic, sugar, ground cumin and pepper. Place chicken in bag and seal. Let chicken marinate in a cooler filled with ice for 1 hour or overnight. Place grilling grate over campfire. Remove chicken pieces from bag. Place chicken on hot grate, skin side down, for about 25 minutes. Turn chicken pieces and cook for an additional 20 to 25 minutes or until the juices run clear and chicken is cooked throughout.

Quick Tip:
Prepare marinade at home and place chicken in bag with marinade. Pack marinating chicken in cooler with ice until ready to prepare recipe.

OUR FAVORITE CHEDDAR BURGER

Makes 4 servings

1 lb. ground beef
⅓ C. steak sauce, divided
4 (1 oz.) slices Cheddar cheese
1 medium onion, cut into strips
1 medium green or red bell
    pepper, cut into strips
1 T. butter or margarine
4 hamburger buns, split
4 slices tomato

Place grilling grate over campfire. In a medium bowl, combine ground beef and 3 tablespoons steak sauce. Mix lightly but thoroughly. Divide mixture into 4 equal parts. Shape each part into a burger, enclosing one slice of Cheddar cheese inside each burger and set aside. Place a skillet on the hot grate and cook onions and bell pepper strips in butter, heating until vegetables are tender. Stir in remaining steak sauce and keep warm. Place burgers on hot grate. Cook burgers over grill for 8 to 10 minutes, turning once, until thoroughly cooked to desired doneness. Remove burgers from grate and place burgers on buns. Top each burger with a tomato slice and some of the cooked onions and peppers.

ON A GRATE

BIG RANCH BURGERS

Makes 4 servings

1 C. sliced onions
⅓ C. sliced green bell pepper strips
⅓ C. sliced red bell pepper strips
1 T. butter or margarine
3 T. A.1. sauce
2 tsp. prepared horseradish
1 lb. ground beef
4 hamburger buns, split

Place grilling grate over campfire. Place a skillet on the hot grate and cook sliced onions, green bell pepper strips and red bell pepper strips in butter, heating until vegetables are tender but crisp. Stir in A.1. sauce and horseradish. Shape ground beef into 4 burgers and place burgers on hot grate. Cook burgers over grill for 8 to 10 minutes, turning once, until thoroughly cooked to desired doneness. Remove burgers from grate and place on buns. Top each burger with ¼ cup of the cooked onions and peppers.

THE ALL-AMERICAN BURGER

Makes 4 servings

1½ lbs. ground beef
2 tsp. Worcestershire sauce
2 T. fresh chopped parsley
2 tsp. onion powder
1 tsp. garlic powder
1 tsp. salt
1 tsp. pepper
4 hamburger buns, split
Ketchup, mustard, chopped
    onions, relish, optional

Place grilling grate over campfire. In a medium bowl, combine ground beef, Worcestershire sauce, chopped parsley, onion powder, garlic powder, salt and pepper. Mix lightly but thoroughly. Shape mixture into four burgers, each about ½" thick. Place burgers on hot grate. Cook burgers over grill for 8 to 10 minutes, turning once, until thoroughly cooked to desired doneness. Remove burgers from grate and place burgers on buns. If desired, garnish burgers with ketchup, mustard, chopped onions and/or relish.

Quick Tip:

Prepare burger mix at home by combining chopped parsley, onion powder, garlic powder, salt and pepper. Pack mixture in an airtight container until ready to prepare recipe. Add ground beef and Worcestershire sauce at campsite.

GRILLED SURF & TURF

Ingredients

4 baking potatoes
1 lb. fresh asparagus, trimmed
2 T. olive oil
Salt and black pepper to taste
12 to 16 oz. frozen scallops,
   thawed and blotted dry
¼ C. butter
4 green onions, sliced
8 oz. fresh mushrooms, sliced
2 tsp. garlic, minced
Vegetable oil
4 tender beef steaks (choose your favorites)

Directions

Wash the potatoes, pierce skins with a fork and wrap tightly in foil. Set them on a grate over a hot fire to cook 45 to 60 minutes or until tender.

Meanwhile, toss asparagus with olive oil and sprinkle with salt and pepper. Insert double skewers through scallops and brush with olive oil; set everything aside. Set a skillet on the grate and melt the butter. Stir in the onions, mushrooms and garlic and sauté until tender; keep warm.

Brush vegetable oil over the exposed grate and arrange steaks on top. Cook to desired doneness, turning once. Partway through cooking time, place asparagus on foil and set on the grate along with scallop skewers. Cook about four minutes, then flip the scallops and asparagus. Cook until scallops are opaque in the middle and asparagus is crisp-tender. When food is done, remove to plates and top steaks with the sautéed mushrooms. Serve with your favorite baked potato toppings, steak sauce and melted butter.

SPINACH ALFREDO PIZZA

Ingredients

4 bacon strips
2 (2.25 oz.) smoked sausages, thinly sliced
1½ C. prepared Alfredo sauce
1 (10 oz.) pkg. frozen chopped spinach,
   thawed and well drained
1 tsp. crushed red pepper flakes
1 (13.8 oz.) tube refrigerated pizza dough
Flour
Olive oil
1 C. shredded Gruyère cheese

Directions

Preheat a grate over hot coals. Gather all topping ingredients so you're ready to add them when the dough begins to cook.

Set a skillet on a grate over a nice fire and fry the bacon and sausage; drain. In the meantime, in another skillet or saucepan, heat the Alfredo sauce and stir in the spinach and pepper flakes. Set everything aside to keep warm.

Unroll the dough on a well-floured cookie sheet and press to ¼" thickness; cut dough into four even pieces. Brush one side of each piece with oil and place on the hot grate, oiled side down. Cook several minutes, until the bottoms are lightly charred. Brush tops with more oil and flip the crusts over onto a clean cookie sheet.

Immediately top with the spinach mixture, spreading it out to within ½" from edges. Add cheese and set-aside sausage and bacon. Return pizzas to the grate and heat several more minutes or until crusts are lightly charred and cooked through and cheese is melted.

INSIDE-OUT CHEESEBURGERS & SWEET CORN

Makes 4 servings

1 lb. lean ground beef
3 T. dry breadcrumbs (such as Italian)
⅓ C. onion, chopped
1 egg
2 tsp. Worcestershire sauce, divided
Salt and black pepper
6 T. shredded Cheddar cheese, divided
1½ T. mayonnaise
½ tsp. prepared yellow mustard
Pickled jalapeños to taste, drained and chopped
4 ears sweet corn
Water
4 hamburger buns, toasted
1 large tomato, thickly sliced
1 large onion, thickly sliced
Butter, softened

Mix the ground beef, breadcrumbs, chopped onion, egg, 1 teaspoon Worcestershire sauce, ½ teaspoon salt and ¼ teaspoon pepper. Shape the mixture into eight patties, about ¼" thick; set aside.

Mix 3 tablespoons cheese, mayonnaise, mustard, jalapeños, ½ teaspoon salt, ¼ teaspoon pepper and remaining 1 teaspoon Worcestershire. Spread mixture evenly on half the hamburger patties to within ½" of the edge; top with remaining cheese and a plain patty.

Seal the edges together well.

Peel back the husks from the sweet corn, without removing them. Remove the silk, sprinkle salt and pepper over the kernels and smooth the husks back in place. Brush husks generously with water.

Set a well-oiled grate over the fire to preheat. Spritz the hamburger patties with cooking spray and place patties and corn on the hot grate. Cook 15 to 20 minutes or until done, turning occasionally. Serve burgers on buns with tomato and onion slices. Husk the corn and serve with butter.

QUICK BACON-AVOCADO PIZZAS

Makes 4 pizzas

4 artisan thin flatbread pizza crusts
Olive oil
½ C. tomato sauce
1½ C. each shredded Cheddar
    and provolone cheeses
6 bacon strips, cooked and chopped
1 or 2 Roma tomatoes, very thinly sliced
Red onion, finely chopped
2 avocados, seeded, peeled, and diced

Make sure all your toppings are ready and by the grate, then preheat the grate over a low-heat fire.

Drizzle the crusts with oil and set them oil-side down on the grate for a couple of minutes, until grill marks appear. Flip them over onto a flat cookie sheet and spread each with about 2 tablespoons of the sauce. Divide half the cheese among the crusts. Top each with the bacon, tomato, onion and avocado, and sprinkle the remaining cheese over all.

Slide the pizzas onto the grate and cook several minutes, until the cheese is melted and grill marks appear on the bottom. Serve hot.

CITRUS SALMON SKEWERS

Makes 4 servings

3 lemons
2 T. fresh parsley, chopped
3 cloves garlic, minced
1½ tsp. Dijon mustard
½ tsp. salt
⅛ tsp. black pepper
2 T. canola oil, plus more for brushing
1 to 1½ lbs. salmon fillets, cut into 1" pieces

Grease the grill grate and preheat the grate on a medium-low heat fire.

Juice one of the lemons and pour the juice into a bowl. Stir in the parsley, garlic, mustard, salt, pepper and 2 tablespoons oil; set aside.

Thinly slice the remaining two lemons. Slide the salmon pieces and lemon slices alternately onto four sets of side-by-side skewers (fold the lemon slices in half). Brush both sides with the mustard mixture.

Set a piece of foil on the grill grates and brush with oil; arrange the skewers on the foil and cook until the salmon is done, turning once.

ROLL OVER BIG DOGS

Makes 8 servings

Olive oil
3 poblano peppers
2 to 3 T. of your favorite mustard
    (we used whole grain)
1 to 2 T. chopped onion
1 to 2 T. salsa
Black pepper to taste
1 (16 oz.) can refried beans, any variety
16 (8") flour tortillas
1 (16 oz.) pkg. shredded Colby Jack cheese
8 (¼ lb.) hot dogs
Cheese dip
Sour cream
Salsa

Grease the grill grate and preheat over a high heat fire.

Drizzle oil over the peppers and set them on the hot grate, cooking until they're nicely charred, turning occasionally. Remove and discard the skin, leaving some of the char in place; coarsely chop the peppers, discarding seeds.

Mix the mustard, onion, salsa, black pepper and beans together and spread evenly over one side of each tortilla. Divide the cheese and chopped peppers over the beans on half the tortillas and stack those on top of the remaining ones, bean sides up; set aside.

Heat the hot dogs on the grate until they're cooked the way you like them. Remove them from the grate, but leave it over the fire. Place a grilled dog on each of the tortilla stacks and roll up to enclose the hot dog tightly inside. Spritz the roll-ups with cooking spray and set them on the grate until they have nice grill marks all around, turning as needed.

Set out cheese dip, sour cream and salsa for dipping.

STUFFED MUSHROOMS

Makes 8 to 10 servings
1 (8 oz.) pkg. fresh mushrooms
2 links fully cooked pork sausage
1 pkg. dry onion soup mix
1 to 2 T. shredded mozzarella cheese

Cover the grate with aluminum foil. Place grilling grate over campfire. Clean mushrooms and twist off caps. Cut cooked pork sausage into small pieces. In a medium bowl, combine dry onion soup mix and pork sausage. Stuff mushroom caps with a generous amount of sausage mixture. Place stuffed mushrooms, cap side down, on aluminum foil on grill. Cook mushrooms over grill for about 15 to 25 minutes. If desired, top stuffed mushrooms with a bit of shredded mozzarella cheese during last few minutes of grilling time. Cook until cheese is melted.

Quick Tip:
Cook pork sausage links at home. Cut into small pieces and mix with dry onion soup mix. Pack mixture in an airtight container and place in cooler until ready to prepare recipe.

TOASTED PESTO ROUNDS

Makes 12 servings
¼ C. fresh chopped basil or dill
¼ C. grated Parmesan cheese
1 clove garlic, minced
3 T. mayonnaise
1 loaf French bread, cut into ¼" thick slices
4 tsp. chopped tomato
1 green onion, sliced
Pepper to taste

Place grilling grate over campfire. In a small bowl, combine chopped basil, grated Parmesan cheese, minced garlic and mayonnaise. Mix well. Lay French bread slices on hot grate for about 1 to 2 minutes, until lightly toasted. Turn slices over and spread an even amount of the mayonnaise mixture over one side of each slice of bread. Top each slice with some of the chopped tomato and sliced green onions. Grill for an additional minute, until bread slices are lightly browned. Season with pepper to taste.

ON A GRATE

POTATO WEDGES

Makes 3 to 4 servings

2 to 3 large potatoes, washed and scrubbed
1 T. olive oil
½ tsp. dried thyme
½ tsp. dried oregano
Salt and pepper to taste

Cover the grate with aluminum foil. Place grilling grate over campfire. Cut potatoes into ⅓" to ½" wedges. Brush potato slices with olive oil and sprinkle with dried thyme and dried oregano. Lay potato wedges over aluminum foil on grill. Sprinkle with salt and pepper to taste. Grill wedges to desired tenderness, turning occasionally.

CORN ON THE COB

Makes 4 servings

4 ears of corn
1½ T. butter, melted
½ tsp. ground cumin
¼ tsp. chili powder
1 tsp. fresh chopped cilantro

Place grilling grate over campfire. Pull back husks from ears of corn, leaving the husks attached. Remove 1 strip of husk from the inner side of each ear of corn and set aside. In a small bowl, combine melted butter, ground cumin, chili powder and chopped cilantro. Brush melted butter mixture onto corn. Bring husks up to cover corn and tie husks together with reserved strips of husk. Place corn cobs on the hot grate and grill for 20 to 30 minutes, turning corn occasionally.

Quick Tip:

To make melted butter mixture, place a small saucepan over grill or fire. Combine butter, ground cumin, chili powder and chopped cilantro in saucepan until melted.

CAMPFIRE FRENCH FRIES

Makes 4 servings

4 potatoes, cut into strips
1 to 2 T. grated Parmesan cheese
Salt and pepper to taste
1 T. butter
2 T. bacon bits

Cover the grate with aluminum foil. Place grilling grate over campfire. Place potato strips in a heavy-duty ziplock bag and add grated Parmesan cheese, salt and pepper. Seal bag and shake until potato strips are covered. Remove potato strips from bag and place on aluminum foil on grill. Dot fries with butter and sprinkle with bacon bits. Cook fries over grill for about 30 to 40 minutes, turning occasionally, until fries are tender.

TENDER CARROT SLICES

Makes 4 servings

4 large carrots, peeled
2 T. olive oil

Cover the grate with aluminum foil. Place grilling grate over campfire. Using a sharp knife, cut carrots in half lengthwise. Brush carrots with olive oil and lay carrots over aluminum foil on grill. Cook carrots to desired tenderness, turning every few minutes.

GRAPEFRUIT EGG CUSTARD

Makes 1 serving

1 grapefruit
1 large egg
2 T. milk
Sugar and cinnamon to taste

Place grilling grate over campfire. Using a sharp knife, slice the top from the grapefruit. Spoon pulp from grapefruit cup and eat or discard, setting aside the grapefruit cup. In a small bowl, whisk together egg and milk. Add sugar and cinnamon to taste. Pour egg mixture into grapefruit cup. Place grapefruit cup on grate, propping with coals to stand up straight, if necessary. Cook over fire or grill until egg is set. Carefully remove grapefruit cup from grill and eat egg directly from grapefruit cup. The grapefruit gives the egg an interesting flavor.

Quick Tip:
Prepare cinnamon and sugar mixture at home by combining ½ tablespoon sugar and ¼ teaspoon cinnamon. Pack in an airtight container until ready to prepare recipe.

Sides

ON A GRATE

STUFFED CHEESE BREAD

Sides

ON A GRATE

Ingredients
- Sourdough loaf
- Mozzarella cheese
- Mushrooms
- Butter, melted
- Garlic powder
- Italian seasoning

Directions
Slice the bread lengthwise and crosswise without cutting through the bottom. Set the loaf in the center of a large double layer of foil sprayed with cooking spray.

Slice cheese and mushrooms and load into cuts. Drizzle butter into the cuts and sprinkle with garlic powder and Italian seasoning.

Seal foil around loaf; set packet in a foil baking pan and place the whole thing on a grate over hot coals. Cook for 20 to 25 minutes or until cheese is melted.

Rotate bread halfway through cooking time. Open packet and serve warm.

CHEESY ROASTED RED PEPPER BREAD

Makes enough for one 1 lb. loaf
- 1 (1 lb.) loaf French bread, unsliced
- 1 C. shredded mozzarella cheese
- ½ C. mayonnaise
- ¼ C. roasted red bell pepper, drained and finely chopped
- ½ tsp. ground cumin
- ¼ C. onion, finely chopped
- 1 T. chopped cilantro, optional

Cut bread horizontally into three layers. In a medium bowl, combine cheese, mayonnaise, bell pepper, cumin, onion and cilantro. Spread on cut sides of bread and wrap in foil. Grill for 15 minutes and serve warm.

FRUIT KEBABS

Makes 6 servings

5 firm bananas, peeled
1 small cantaloupe, seeded and rind removed
12 large firm strawberries, stemmed
¼ C. butter, melted
2 T. fresh lime juice
1 T. honey

Preheat grill to medium heat. Cut bananas and cantaloupe into 1½" chunks. Thread on skewers alternately with strawberries. Combine butter, lime juice and honey; brush kebabs with mixture and place on grill. Cook about 5 minutes on each side, brushing occasionally with butter mixture. Serve immediately. If using wooden skewers, be sure to soak in water at least 30 minutes before using to prevent burning.

BACON-WRAPPED ASPARAGUS

Makes 4 to 6 servings

24 asparagus spears
Black pepper to taste
12 strips of bacon, cut in half crosswise

Place asparagus on a sheet of waxed paper; coat with cooking spray. Sprinkle with black pepper; turn to coat. Wrap bacon around each spear; secure ends with toothpicks. Grill bacon-wrapped asparagus, uncovered for 4 to 6 minutes on each side or until bacon is crisp.

BACON & CORN STUFFED PEPPERS

Makes 4 servings

2 C. frozen corn, thawed
⅓ C. salsa
6 green onions, chopped
1 medium green bell pepper, halved, seeds and membranes removed
1 medium red bell pepper, halved, seeds and membranes removed
¼ C. shredded mozzarella cheese
2 bacon strips, cooked and crumbled
Additional salsa, optional

Preheat grate over medium heat fire. In a large bowl, combine corn, salsa and onions; spoon mixture into bell pepper halves. Grill to desired doneness. Sprinkle with cheese and bacon. Return to grate for 3 to 5 minutes or until cheese is melted. Serve with additional salsa, if desired.

ON A GRATE

ATOMIC POPPERS

Makes 20 poppers

10 jalapeños
1 (8 oz.) pkg. cream cheese spread
1 C. finely shredded Monterey Jack cheese
1 tsp. chipotle powder
2 green onions, finely chopped
20 mini smoked sausages
20 bacon slices, cooked

Preheat the the grate over medium-low heat fire. Slice jalapeños in half lengthwise; remove and discard the seeds and membranes. (Always be careful prepping jalapeños—these beasts can do a number on your skin and eyes.)

Mix cream cheese spread with Monterey Jack cheese, chipotle powder and green onions; stuff into the pepper halves. Nestle a mini smoked sausage into the filling of each and wrap a bacon strip around the whole thing. Secure with toothpicks and set them on the grate; cover with foil and cook several minutes, until the peppers are slightly tender and lightly charred and the filling is piping hot.

ALMOST STIR-FRY RICE

Makes 4 servings

1⅓ C. uncooked instant rice
⅓ C. fresh mushrooms, sliced
¼ C. green bell pepper, chopped
¼ C. onion, chopped
½ C. chicken stock
⅓ C. ketchup
½ C. water
Salt and black pepper to taste
1 T. butter

Preheat the grate over a medium heat fire. In a greased 9" round foil pan, stir together instant rice, mushrooms, bell pepper, onion, chicken stock, ketchup, water and salt and black pepper to taste. Dot with butter. Cover with greased foil and seal the edges tightly.

Set the pan on the grate and heat for 12 to 15 minutes or until the liquid is absorbed and the rice is tender. Be careful when lifting that foil cover—the steam inside will be hot.

ROCKY TRAIL HIKING MIX

Makes 5½ cups

3 C. frosted mini wheat squares
½ C. raisins or currants
½ C. sunflower seeds, shelled
½ C. pumpkin seeds, shelled
½ C. dried mixed fruit
½ C. M&M's
½ tsp. salt, optional

In a large bowl, combine frosted mini wheat squares, raisins, sunflower seeds, pumpkin squares, dried mixed fruit, M&M's and salt. Toss gently with hands until evenly incorporated. Pack mixture in a large ziplock bag.

CRAN-GORP

Makes 5 cups

½ C. mixed nuts
½ C. macadamia nuts
1 C. dried cranberries or craisins
1 C. M&M's
1 C. sunflower seeds, shelled

In a large bowl, combine mixed nuts, macadamia nuts, dried cranberries, M&M's and sunflower seeds. Toss gently with hands until evenly incorporated. Pack mixture in a large ziplock bag.

CAMPING CRUNCH

Makes 10 cups

7 C. crispy rice cereal
1 C. mini pretzel sticks
1 C. bite-size cheese crackers
1 C. cashews or peanuts
¼ C. margarine, melted
½ tsp. garlic salt
½ tsp. onion salt
2½ tsp. lemon juice
5 tsp. Worcestershire sauce

Preheat oven to 450°F. In a large bowl, combine crispy rice cereal, mini pretzel sticks, cheese crackers and cashews. Mix well with hands. Place butter in a glass measuring cup. Melt butter in microwave and pour over dry ingredients. Sprinkle with garlic salt, onion salt, lemon juice and Worcestershire sauce and mix well. Spread mixture evenly into an 11" x 17" jellyroll pan. Bake mixture in oven for 45 to 60 minutes, stirring after every 15 minutes. Remove pan from oven and spread mixture onto paper towels to dry. Pack mixture in a large ziplock bag.

CAFE BAVARIAN MINT MIX

Makes 8 servings
¼ C. powdered creamer
⅓ C. sugar
¼ C. instant coffee granules
2 T. cocoa powder
2 hard mint candies, crushed

In a medium bowl, combine powdered creamer, sugar, instant coffee granules, cocoa powder and crushed mint candies. Toss gently with hands until evenly incorporated. Pack mixture in a large ziplock bag. At campsite, mix 2 tablespoons coffee mixture with 1 to 1½ cups hot water.

SWISS MOCHA MIX

Makes 6 servings
6 T. powdered milk
3 T. instant coffee granules
3 T. sugar
1¼ tsp. cocoa powder

In a medium bowl, combine powdered milk, instant coffee granules, sugar and cocoa powder. Toss gently with hands until evenly incorporated. Pack mixture in a large ziplock bag. At campsite, mix 2 tablespoons coffee mixture with 1 to 1½ cups hot water.

FIRESIDE GRANOLA

Ingredients
1½ C. chopped pecans
4 C. quick-cooking oats
½ C. brown sugar
¼ tsp. cinnamon
¼ tsp. salt
⅓ C. coconut oil
¼ C. honey
1 T. maple syrup

Directions
Layer two 18" lengths of heavy-duty foil and grease well. Dump pecans, oats and brown sugar onto foil and sprinkle with cinnamon and salt. Mix well. Stir in coconut oil and seal foil around granola, pressing pack flat. Set on a grate over hot coals for 10 to 15 minutes to brown, turning and shaking pack occasionally. Drizzle granola with honey and maple syrup. Stir and let cool.

WIDE-EYED COLD BREW

Makes 8 servings
½ C. ground coffee
Water
Ice
Half-and-half
Sweetened condensed milk

The night before, put ground coffee into a 1-quart mason jar; fill the jar with water, cover, and let set overnight at room temperature.

The next morning, strain through cheesecloth into a clean mason jar; discard coffee grounds. Add water to the coffee to fill the jar.

To serve, fill a 1-pint jar with ice; fill ⅔ full with the coffee. Add a big splash of half-and-half and sweetened condensed milk to taste. Stir before serving.

Methods of Keeping Animals from Getting to Your Food

Whenever you are camping, you'll want to consider where you will store your food so that wild animals do not visit your camp in search of food. Keep the following guidelines in mind, and be sure to supplement them with advice from rangers or other authorities in your camping area.

- Never leave your food, even if it's still in your pack, unattended.
- Empty your pack overnight, and leave all pockets and compartments open. This way, nocturnal visitors can snoop around without being tempted to gnaw at or shred your gear to see what's inside.
- Cook meals and store food at least 100 feet away from your sleeping area. Keep food in airtight containers to help contain the smell. Anything with a heavy aroma—powder, ointment, toothpaste, sunscreen, bug spray, lotion—should also be stored with your food, as animals are drawn to any exotic smells. Keep the stash downwind of your site, if possible.
- Use bear boxes, bear wires, or bear poles if available.
- Alternate your hiding place; don't use the same place every time. Animals are creatures of habit and will come back to the same places in search of food. You'll also want to avoid using the same tree other campers have already used.
- Keep a clean camp. The best way to prevent animals from visiting your campsite is to not give them any incentives to come or to stay.
- Never feed a wild animal.

INDEX

Recipes by Title Index

Meat or Main Ingredient Index